The Millennial Mentality

More than Memes, Cats & Mishaps

Elan M. Carson

www.elanmcarson.com

Ordering Information:

Quantity sales. Special discounts are available on quantity purchases by corporations, associations, and others. For details, contact the publisher at the web address above.

Printed in the United States of America

Edited by Kim Huther, Jennifer Olson, and Elan Carson

Cover Design by PixelStudio

Cover Illustration by antalogiya@hotmail.com

Photography by Clarke (Latta) Henry III

For Grandma Jones,

Mr. Kitty

(he will claim that he really wrote this book),

Mom & Pat Geary

Table of Contents

The Millennial Mentality

More than Memes, Cats & Mishaps

Elan M. Carson

Introduction

Why I Wrote This Book

Millennials are the most misunderstood generation of our time and I want to change that. We are often characterized as lazy, entitled narcissists, and poor workers who bounce from one career role to the next. From the lens of a Millennial, I challenge that we are the complete opposite. We are the do-gooders who confront traditional belief systems and bring awareness to social norms that need reformation. We are the free spirits not married to making a high income, but for living life fully and happily. And we are the creatives, who like meaningful and life-changing projects to drive our success in the midst of our oftentimes blurred work and life "balance."

Everyone likes an underdog story, and that's why I wrote this book. Millennials are that underdog. Bred as over-achievers since kindergarten, we have struggled to find footing in traditional workplaces. We have struggled to date. We have struggled to pay off student loans that exist in the trillions. We have struggled to survive as adults in general, hence the phrase "delayed adulthood." But we have also succeeded, and our successes have been big victories.

We've pioneered new and more positive ways to work, creating workspaces that offer increased flexibility, autonomy, and peer-to-peer collaboration. We're changing the way other generations look at the world by protesting things that are important to us, like body image inclusivity for people of all shapes and sizes, race-relations domestically and across the globe, and the unfair treatment of women, from the lower wages earned in Western cultures to the denial of girls receiving education in developing nations. In this way, Millennials are revolutionaries, thought-leaders, and a generation of activists.

I want our story as Millennials to be told, and I want a chance to undo the negative stereotypes. We were thrown into the myriad rules of adulthood ruled by tradition, systemic institutions, and cookie-cutter socializations. Now, as we change the landscape of what it means to be an adult, we have the chance to change other generations' outlook on the world as well. And that is something worth noting and vying for. I wanted our story told because we are not the "Me" generation, but the "Why Not Me" generation, and that is what makes us worth reading and learning about.

Who is Generation-Y?

Bemoaned as a generation of entitlement and nicknamed the Internet Generation and the Boomerang Generation (among others), we have heard all of the cultural criticisms and backlash about our transition into adulthood. But we have made it through that knothole, sometimes being strung through backwards, crossing into the threshold of our mid-twenties and early thirties.

A lot has changed, and we have inspired a lot of these changes. Believed to be the "gayest" generation[1]—or the generation with the most openly gay people—we are tolerant of everyone loving whomever they happen to love. We are reshaping race relations in response to hundreds of Black Americans being beaten to death by law enforcement, disenfranchised, and let down by the myth of a post-racial society.

We are challenging standards for women's equality and the surmounting media culture that encourages an unhealthy body image. And, interestingly, as the Internet Generation, we're accomplishing this by way of social media protests, or what was once considered Slacktivism, in addition to countrywide riots. We are informing our own nation, as well as those abroad, about unjust policies and discriminatory traditions using Facebook, Twitter, Instagram, Snapchat and others to satisfy our need for immediate action.

Yes, our value systems have changed. Yes, our beliefs have expanded to be more inclusive. Yes, our life goals have shifted to prioritize happiness over workplace cubicles in gray-scale offices. Our ROI in higher education, a value proposition promising us if we worked hard we would be rewarded, failed us. Our caps, gowns, and diplomas lost their promised value, and were stripped of merit as we entered an economically dilapidated workforce during a historically low recession. It is no secret that the majority of us limped away from our education. A ball and chain of student loan debt in the trillions keeps us from the stable life we used to dream of before the name Sallie Mae became our uncomfortable wake up call into adulthood, with no option to hit snooze.

To those who knew us as the Boomerang Generation, at first we could not afford to move out of our parents' homes, but the businesses we started on our journey to find inspiring work shows our penchant for leadership, entrepreneurship, and innovation. For those who credited us as the Generation of Entitlement, of course we felt privileged to experience the success promised to us, when what we really worked toward was an elusive American Dream based on a faulty reward system. We scrambled to change the landscape of success, and we are vehemently working to realign the system to work for and with us. We are Generation-Y, a culture of tech-innovators, policy-changers, counter-culture-bohemians, always-in-transit-hipsters, and, most importantly, informed citizens.

We may not be homeowners with 2.5 children, grasping mid-rung on a corporate ladder, but we are cat-owners, adaptable to change, creatively crowdfunding ways to champion our projects and goals. No more busy work that relates little to our talents for a pay bump and title change with limited perks and benefits. Our startups will instead revolutionize workplace tradition by way of more flexibility, peer-to-peer opportunities to learn, and unlimited vacation days.

So, while we are binge-watching our favorite new diversity-inclusive television shows on Netflix, like *Orange is the New Black* or anything by the multi-talented Shonda Rhimes, starting our own business modeled after non-traditional practices, or advocating for more social equality in every facet of our lives, we are also fighting to accomplish our own individual dreams to support ourselves. The dreams that made us work hard in the first place. We are Millennials, and we're changing the way you see the world, while inventing the future.

Why You Need This Book

This book covers information about one of the world's most interesting and dynamic generations: Generation-Y or, more precisely, Millennials. Studies circulate regularly covering Gen-Y habits: from our spending and budgeting tactics to why we are marrying later, or waiting to buy homes. Reports even discuss our work ethics, oftentimes in a negative light. I cover these subjects, plus more, with a different take. As a Millennial, I look at the different things that affect our behavior and motivate our actions. I also share comedic anecdotes, providing a wider lens.

Millennials are the most fascinating generation to cover because we have so much to lose, but also the most to gain. As we disrupt traditional standards, create a more culturally inclusive society, and use our hyper-connectivity to initiate online protests and strategize social justice movements, our restructuring is creating the optimal time for change and revolution. This correlates with advancements in technology and the Web space, like mobile evolutions and social media.

Being a technologically savvy generation, or Digital Natives[2], we aim for constant and instant social connectivity, merging the different facets of our lives. Sometimes, this can play out haphazardly, leading to social mishaps along the way, or sometimes we can create immediacy…urgency, giving life to a new protest with hashtag activism. We're more connected than ever and we know this empowers us.

Learn what it is like to live, eat, breathe, and sleep Millennial, the poorest generation of overachievers you will meet. Each chapter starts off with a surprising fact about the subject matter at hand and is denoted as "Truth Bomb," and ends with a list of information that pinpoints specific facts, events, and movements that were not included in the chapter. This means, even if you are a Millennial, you can still find bits of information helpful like discovering the difference between income-based repayment and income-contingent repayment, learning about impactful social justice movements, or reading how, even after electing a Black president, we haven't made it to a Utopian post-racial society despite beliefs that we have.

If you aren't a Millennial, discover what we need as employees. Learn about the cultural revolutions we're sparking including the need for women's equality worldwide, inclusive LGBT+ rights, body image positivity, and more. Our undying infatuation with cats, our obsession with Harry Potter, and our love of selfies are a few quirks that capture the day-to-day life of Millennials, when we are not working to change the world for the better. Even if you're just curious about Millennial culture, you'll find something new to give you a fresh outlook on this again and again misperceived generation.

Who Am I?

I am a cat lover, activist, and most importantly, a writer who relishes in telling great stories. The Generation-Y narrative is significant to me because I grew up in a time period where pulling all-nighters, getting straight A's, and signing up for extracurriculars was necessary in order to earn acceptance into a notable college. Rinse and repeat the same process at university, and I was told that I could land a job in my desired career field with a decent pay. Fast-forward almost a decade, and the job market is only now starting to recover.

Finally, I can start a savings account, as well as put money away in a 401K. I'm also now working in an exciting and meaningful role, while having enough funds to pay off that pricey college tuition after years of having low wages and uninspiring work. Talk about a delay!

My being part of Generation-Y, a generation that prides itself on having information and accessing that information instantaneously, means that I am part of a larger culture that wants to see positive and consistent change. We acknowledge that, in some facets of Western culture, reform is imminent.

As a Millennial, I have lived to see a Black American occupy a spot as President while simultaneously witnessing the persistent and systemic racism. I've lived to see the federal legalization of gay marriage, and watched LGBT+ friends revel in the excitement of liberty while the suicide rates for LGBT+ teens have endured.

I've lived to see advances in technology that seems to be happening at unquantifiable speeds—from my first Barbie computer in the 90s to my touch-screen tablet today, while developing countries are still working to access things like running water and working electricity. I've lived to experience the beginning of shifts in media to include body-positive messaging, inspiring me and many other women to be confident, regardless of size, to try to counteract eating disorders like anorexia and bulimia that are rampant. I have lived through many changes, but, as a Millennial, I know there is still so much more our culture can do to create a forward-thinking progressive and inclusive society. And I want to be part of that change. I am Elan Carson and I am a radical, do-gooder, creative-thinking Millennial with a story to share.

1

It's Complicated

Truth Bomb:

According to a Pew Research study "5 Facts about Online Dating," published in 2015, only 5% of Americans who are married or in a committed relationship credit finding their partner online, even when examining couples who have been together five years or fewer.[1]

—

When it came down to it, I preferred OKCupid to PlentyofFish. The design's modernity, pink and navy color combination, and user-friendly profile layouts were in sync with my Type A personality. Every couple of weeks I would update my profile to make sure the refreshes kept my page in site searches. Next came the waiting. I would typically receive messages fairly quickly, but none from the lovelorn like myself. Men like "Reclez" who would attempt to entice me with a "What's up" or "Heyyy," prodding around my profile. Or there were those who would send thoughtful messages, but never wanted to meet in person. After months of keeping a chat conversation going, I deduced I was most likely being catfished.

Despite these social mishaps and others that came along with online dating, such as receiving the infamous penis pictures, taciturn chat responses, and ab selfies, friends continually encouraged me to use dating websites and apps. I loved hearing success stories from them, and that kept me engaged one weird date after another. Soon, my dating stories became a source of amusement and inspired teasing from them. They realized that, with my luck, online dating was a crapshoot.

One of my first online dating encounters was with a not-so-gentlemanly person who I will call Joe. Joe and I arranged to see each other at a lounge in the hip-ish area of Los Angeles, nicknamed SoRo for the South Robertson area. Afro-funk music eclipsed our ability to have a conversation at first, but when we finally got the chance to talk, he shared that he was a business owner of a tech startup. This was promising: a man with a career. Plus, the writer in me loves a good conversationalist, and Joe was a talksmith. We chatted for hours, leaning in to catch what the other was saying, giggling at our awkward poses and posture.

He even bought me sliders, my favorite dish. The first hour passed by and everything was seemingly normal. However, later into our rendezvous, there was a shift in his behavior. He would encourage me to drink more and talk less. Frequently, he would leave me seated to go to the bar and purchase more drinks, even if I wasn't finished with the last. He would tease I couldn't keep up with him, and I forced myself to chug Vodka lemonade in an effort to seem both cool and polite–every woman's downfall: politesse. By the fourth drink, I called it quits. He casually invited me back to his place to watch him play guitar. I declined, stating I was tired, but countered that we could meet for another outing later in the week. Terse, he left me on the street corner to wait for an Uber at 1:00 a.m.

Did men only want one thing? The hackneyed saying television moms tout ran through my thoughts. I never heard back from Joe, who just wanted to hook up with so little time passing between our first meeting and getting intimate.

Over the next year, I continued online dating, enlisting the help of a dating coach similar to the movie *Hitch* to help me weed out potential duds. Eventually, I tapped into PlentyofFish and Match.com, realizing that siloing myself on OKCupid would only narrow the dating pool. I even tried JDate, since I'm a sucker for Jewish men. None of these efforts panned into anything meaningful, however. Date after date, the men I met seemed clueless, or maybe I wasn't clued in to the dating game. Either way, I had a lot of nights where what I envisioned did not go according to plan.

One guy immediately felt me up after the introductory hug, and did not resist the opportunity to sneak in other touches throughout our conversation. Another just wanted to take pictures of me as he toted around his expensive, professional-grade camera and lens, while yet another blatantly told me my boobs weren't as big as my heart. How come I wasn't shaping up to be a success story like my friend, engaged to her PlentyofFish find? I didn't want a casual fling; I wanted love promised to me by these matchmaking sites and their sophisticated algorithms.

My experiences solidified that, as a Millennial, I was in the age of the hook-up culture; hook-up culture being common for both men and women to publically decry that they want some action. When online dating and dating apps took prevalence, Millennials took out the courtship that came along with romance, shortening the length of time between getting to know someone and ultimately hooking-up.

Sociology Professor Ida Cook prolifically notes, "There's a different mindset among young people today, in part because they're experiencing a kind of extended childhood. I would call it serial mating. It gives that generation more time to explore when, in decades past, they would have been expected to get married and have children."[2]

Ideas of having a long-term relationship are mixed, especially for those who solely want to build their career first before starting a family, or even Millennials who are leery of jumping into a committed relationship so early in their lives after witnessing parents' divorce. These change of ideas where we are waiting longer to settle down also inspire shifts in how we date. There are no flowers, picking up the dinner tab, or walk in the park wind down, traditional strategies my Gen-Xer friends implemented to court. I was lucky to get a courtesy text, pursuant of meeting someone. Here I was, using obsolete tactics that were only as relevant as the last John Hughes flick, in an era where postponing marriage or even long-term commitment is normal. It was time for me to accept the rules of modern dating, which included my first "It's Complicated" relationship.

An Australian with a penchant for getting into trouble was my first foray into "it's complicated" territory and I learned a lot. The idea of hooking up with someone without the unnecessary pressure of a relationship meant I could explore myself with him intimately, and still be independent. I didn't feel the pressure from family when they asked why I wasn't in a relationship, when I could state that I *was* seeing someone. I was free to flake on a weekend of hanging out and, when I did want to participate in a "night out with the guys," I could because I wasn't the intrusive girlfriend.

Neither of us wanted to get hurt after our tough dating experiences and we settled for just sex. It was selfish and uncomplicated, though our "it's-complicated" label ironically categorized our relationship. Our hook-ups without commitment lasted for a year, and I even tossed around the idea of what would happen if I proposed having a conventional "boyfriend/girlfriend" label, the kind that involved updating my Facebook profile with the symbolic red heart time stamping our affections.

Would he find someone else who was more easy-going or would he agree that maybe we needed more than a middle-of-the-road moniker? We'll never know, however, as he eventually moved back to Australia. His and my ineptitude to commit maybe kept us from being truly vulnerable with each other. And, though I would like to believe our connection was special, we both were as engaged with each other as we were disengaged. We still sought out other options, but kept the other on speed dial in case we faced rejection.

Many Millennials witnessed marital instability in our home lives. Data from the 2010 Pew Research study *The Decline of Marriage And Rise of New Families* reveals that in 1960, 87% of children under age 18 lived in a home with both parents. By 2008, that number dropped to 64%. During the same time period, children born to unmarried women increased from 5% to 41%.[3] From what society tells Gen-Y, marriages will end with divorce courts, custody battles, and the disharmonious splitting of assets. Nothing seems amicable about jumping into marriage so soon as prior generations did. This has participated in us wanting to A/B test different suitors without the promise of something longer, unless we wanted it to be.

After my "it's complicated" relationship, I attempted to revisit the online dating world. Eventually, I unplugged, however, realizing an excessive amount of options via matchmaking sites didn't help me find someone better. It made the act of choosing more difficult. I remained stuck in the "paradox of choice"[4] these applications and websites provided. As Millennials continue to redefine and modify our standards in the quest to find someone compatible, a Gen-Yer's decision about whom to pursue becomes seemingly endless. In fact, according to the Pew Research report *Online Dating and Relationships*, 32% of Internet users agreed with the statement that "online dating keeps people from settling down because they always have options for people to date."[5]

Once I opted out of matchmaking services, my friend's brother, the friend engaged to her PlentyofFish find, and I realized we had a connection. He and I used Facebook to later connect, which soon progressed into texting, then phone calls, and eventually dating. More than a hook up or "it's complicated" scenario, we ventured into caring about each other. We enjoyed each other's company and conversation, spent a considerable amount of time together, and alternated between who would pick up the tab for dinner. If an emergency happened, we could rely on each other for support or late night phone calls. Lincoln and Illana's relationship from the comedic television show *Broad City* is a perfect example of this. Even though we never formalized our relationship with a girlfriend/boyfriend title, we spent the next half year as dating partners, a term writer Kate Hakala explains in her article *20-Somethings Have Invented a New Relationship Status...*[6] before he fulfilled his plans to move to Germany to pursue affordable education and a better career.

Overall, what does the future look like for romance and Millennials? Tech-enabled dating sites continue to evolve. With easy-to-navigate platforms that know so much about us, they can generate a profile of "the one," or many others if the first one doesn't work out. And while some of us aren't jumping into long-term commitments as quickly as generations prior, our short-term engagements can help us discover what we value intimately, what our priorities are, and who will ultimately be the best fit to end our hook-up culture phenomenon. In short, while we pursue the right partner, dating in the digital era can best be described as "it's complicated."

Five Dating Don'ts (Culminated Mostly from Equally Bad & Comical Experiences)

1) Never admit to your date that they are your back-up option because your first choice bailed.

2) Avoid talking about past relationship failures and/or exes obsessively for the entire span of the date.

3) Stay away from attempting to coax an inebriated date into hooking up, unless they plainly and verbally express consent before drinking. Even then they still have the right to say no. Flirting or flirtatious comments from your date, as well as how your date is dressed, does not automatically express consent to engage in sexual activity.

4) Although texting is a quick way of communication, don't let this type of messaging be the only form of exchange between you and a potential partner. Pick up the phone and call. As expert millionaire matchmaker Patti Stanger often reminds her clients, hearing someone's voice is arousing and intimate.

5) If you are not interested in a person after meeting them, avoid fading away (like the Garfunkel and Oates song...yes this is a real comedy-folk duo!) or "Ghosting," (see chapter 14 on Millennial Slang) and

just openly let the person know they're not your type.

2

Cat-titude of Gratitude

Truth Bomb:

According to ASPCA® approximately 7.6 million animals enter shelters nationwide each year. Of those, roughly 3.9 million are dogs and 3.4 million are cats.[1] Don't have a furry friend? Whether cat, dog, or bunny, adopt the newest member of your family today and help save a life.

—

Draped under my quilted cover, I tried my hardest not to move. It was 6:00 a.m. and my cat's jaunty meows were sounding off before my alarm. I could feel him leap sprightly over my resting body, trying to figure out where I was tucked in. Curiously, he investigated for any clues that I was awake and ready to play, any slight movement tipping him off that I was conscious. He found the top of my head, pawing jovially, before releasing another loud meow—near my ear this time—and jumping off the bed to go find another source of amusement. Slightly agitated, but even more subdued by his cuteness, I went back to sleep, but only for an hour before Mr. Kitty returned.

Author of *We Learn Nothing*, Tim Kreider comically describes the relationship between human and cat best in his essay cleverly titled *A Man and His Cat*. "I LIVED with the same cat for 19 years—by far the longest relationship of my adult life. Under common law, this cat was my wife."[2]

Mr. Kitty is *my* partner-in-crime (I often refer to him as the beauty and me the brains), slothful roommate, and, in fact, the longest relationship I had ever had. After 13 years of living together, he understands my idiosyncrasies just as I get his passive-aggression; thus we make the perfect team.

Knowing that I consider my cat to be part of my inner social circle of friends may seem strange, but cats have already taken over the Internet world. Dominating our everyday lives with cuteness seems only fair. Celebricats (celebrity cats, not to be confused with cats of celebrities, which I will cover later) are more than in vogue; they are capitalizing on quirks, imperfections, and unique features. Tardar Sauce, better known as Grumpy Cat because of her scowl, for example, has amassed millions with help from a movie, book, and branded merchandise. Other A-list felines[3] from Lil Bub, suffering from genetic mutations and osteoporosis, to Nala, credited for looking curious and surprised reminiscent of Taylor Swift's surprised face at award shows, have robust social media followings, product lines, and fan art to solidify their claim to fame. Millennials, including me, are just that obsessed.

Day in and day out, friends and I text each other personal photos, quotes, and memes, including content often shared from Caturday.[4] We consider Pusheen our favorite sticker who absolutely understands the value of capturing the right emotion—Pusheen on a Scooter Bicycle gets our free spiritedness.[5] And we send each other listicles from BuzzFeed ("Cat people are 25% likely to pick George as their favorite Beatle" notes Chelsea Marshall, in her post *82 Astounding Facts About Cats*[6]). Even the story of Craig Armstrong and his feline hiking buddy named Millie, circuited Facebook and Twitter, reaching over 80,000 likes on the leading art, design, and photography site BoredPanda.[7]

Celebrities are as crazy about their cats as we are, reiterating that cats have earned their reign in the kingdom of cuteness beside puppies and unicorns. Choupette Lagerfeld–adopted by Karl Lagerfeld–has two handmaids to assist with beauty prepping and to keep track of her daily activities in a diary, for example.

Taylor Swift, nicknamed the "Patron Saint of Cats" by friend Lena Dunham, has two feline friends, Olivia Benson and Meredith Grey, and they are frequently the subject of her social media posts. Ian Somerhalder is another celebrity fond of cats, and has posed with his buddy Moke for *People* magazine. Similar to Swift, his Instagram followers are treated to impromptu photo shoots of the duo.

In addition to owning cats and sharing our favorite four-legged moments on social media channels, Millennials attribute to the popularity of events such as the first-ever Cat Convention, along with the success of businesses like Cat Cafés. CatConLA, held in Los Angeles the summer of 2015, welcomed 10,000 visitors and cat lovers. The two-day weekend event focused on cat-centric design and art ideas, developments, and products, as well as welcoming celebrities, celebricats, and merchandise to further create a climate centered on cat culture. Part of the money from ticket prices went to benefit a non-profit organization, FixNation, aimed at reducing cat homelessness. Cat Cafés and lounges are other booming businesses, offering cat lovers the opportunity to find retreat amongst a room full of cats, while enjoying tea or a cappuccino. There's even the option to adopt after the experience.

On a typical day, I'm either crabby from trying to get Mr. Kitty to play with his new premium scratching post, only to later discover he's more content to engage with the packaging and wrappings in battle, or my cat's desultory kindness leads to the thought that maybe he's plotting to kill me. Today, I tried to beat him at his own game of shrewdness, however. I approached Mr. Kitty with a convivial spirit, that akin to a dog. He was crouched atop his favorite book, painfully trying to avoid eye contact as I made faux antennae with my arms, buzzing about the room to catch his attention. Oh, how the tables have turned from earlier this morning before sunrise, when he had ached for a playmate. Now it was my turn to be the mischievous pest. Slowly, but surely, he relented to my coos, initially squinty-eyed with malice, but now more affectionate. He arched his back to stand, leapt from his resting place, and whipped his tail around my leg to signify a hug before eventually settling next to me. We plopped together on the couch, and I verbalized, "I win, Mr. Kitty. Until the next morning."

Six Conversations this Millennial Has With Her Cat

1. On Choosing a Going Out Look:

Cat Owner (me): Mr. Kitty, I need help picking out an outfit today, and STAT. Do you think I should go with the lace-hemmed purple tutu?

Cat: *blank stare*

Me: Don't be so rude. I'll chalk that up to a "no." How about the leopard print top and gray booties? Totally *me-ow*, right?

Cat: *Tilts head to the left*

Me: You're being so difficult right now, and I have to leave in twenty. Plus, you didn't even laugh at my cat joke. Fine, what about this fuzzy pink cat sweater and metallic white skirt?

Cat: *Imperceptible flick of tail*

Me: Score! Knew you'd like that one!

2. On Friday Nights:

Me: So everyone is staying in tonight; at least I can say you're my Friday night date, Mr. Fluffy Poodles. P.S. Don't you like my new nickname for you?

Cat: *Blinks regretfully*

Me: Hopefully, you didn't have plans to party with the cat next door. That would be a real bummer.

Cat: *Yawns*

Me: If I'm boring you, Mr. Kitty, we can watch TV in separate rooms.

Cat: …

Me: Fine, I'm going to order a pizza and we'll just forget this happened.

Mom calls

Mom: How's your Friday?

Me: Just watching a movie with my date.

3. On Halloween:

Me: I think I'm dressing up as a sexy cat this year!

Cat: *Rolls over*

Me: So cheeky, right? You are my muse, Mr. Kitty.

Cat: *Flicks tail lovingly*

Me: Ok, I know this is the elephant in the room. Your vampire Halloween costume didn't end well last year. How about a mermaid? They have a sweet deal at the pet store where it comes with a clip-on wig and seashell pasties!

Cat: *Narrows eyes*

Me: Fine, the lobster is also a cute option! Everyone will love it.

Cat: *Narrows eyes to death stare*

Me: No costume for kitty this year.

4. Cleaning:

Me: I'm going to be home late today; would you mind tidying up?

Cat: *Curled on pillow*

Me: Just asking you to take out the trash and make up the bed...

Cat: *Closes eyes to go back to sleep*

Me: What, are you a supermodel now? Since when do you not get out of bed for less than ten grand?

Cat: *Blissfully ignores cat owner*

Me: Such a diva; you've been listening to too much Beyoncé.

5. On Borrowing Clothes:

Me: Did you wear my suede pumps again? There's fur all over them!

Cat: *Cleans front paw*

Me: Poodles, how many times have I told you to use the lint roller when you're done borrowing my clothes?

Cat: *Pauses licking front paw*

Me: I am not your maid kitty!

Cat: *Commences cleaning paws and face*

Me: I'll let it go this time only because you're so cute.

6. On Ignoring Me:

Me: Kitty, do you still love me?

Cat: *Slow blink*

Me: Today you didn't even come out of the cupboard, and when I tried to squeeze in you just turned around and pretended I didn't exist.

Cat: *Closes eyes*

Me: Is this because I don't pay enough attention to you? I have a life, too, Poodles.

Cat: *Slaps me in the face with fluffy, long-haired tail*

Me: Thanks for the sass, Mr. Kitty.

3

HOA TO DOA:
Getting out of Debt is the New American Dream

Truth Bomb:

In 2014, student loans made up 36.8% of total debt for the age group 20-29, noted in a study conducted by TransUnion.[1]

—

I am part of the growing 70% of Millennials[2] who have a bloated amount of student loan debt to pay back, and I am kicking myself. I remember the adamant words of my mother encouraging me while I was still in school to finish college early and start paying off loans while I was studying to get my degree. By the start of this paragraph, you can already tell I did not follow her advice.

In 2015, five years after the recession, Millennials had amassed over $1.3 trillion in student loan debt, surpassing credit card debt and auto loans. Nearly three-quarters of us walked away with approximately $33,000 in debt after only obtaining a Bachelor's degree. This number is up from $18,650, the average amount of debt a person would graduate with in the year 2004.[3] Combine Gen-Yers' student loans with a still-wavering job market, and our post-college experience becomes a matter of financial sink or swim.

A mid-Westerner, there were only two things in life that I wanted at the age of 17: to go to college and to go to college in California. I was persistent at convincing my mother to join me on the opposite side of the country. This wasn't too hard to do, seeing as how the economy in 2007 was hurting, and Detroit in particular was a city that seemed to get the really short end of the stick. Before packing up and leaving, both my mom and I secured the university I would be attending in the fall. What I did not realize was that, although I had been accepted into a private liberal arts school, not all educational institutions were created equal.

The money I would borrow for perks, such as a low number of students to faculty ratio, customized education, and a strong writing program, didn't guarantee that I would be able to secure a job after college to pay back loans. Additionally, the degree I was getting would not equate to a competitive paying job immediately after graduating. The ten most popular majors, starting at Business Administration and ending at History, with Psychology and Accounting in between, were not degrees employers in booming job markets were seeking.[4] According to consulting company Adecco, 75% of the fastest-growing occupations require math skills, and other flourishing industries necessitate science, technology, or engineering aptitude; the latter combining to create STEM skills.[5]

Semester after semester, for all four years of college, I would get a phone call from my mom, increasingly worried about the rising costs of tuition. The first year, since I was attending as an out-of-state student, was undoubtedly the most expensive. My mom and I expected the cost to drop, which it did at first, but, as the economy on the national level continued to tank, tuition prices were hiked as faculty and staff members were being let go. By 2009-10, departments at my particular university were being slashed, favored professors were saying goodbye, classroom sizes were losing their coveted low student to faculty ratio, and the cost of attendance was becoming a heavy financial burden. In essence, everything that I was paying for, I was losing, and other colleges, both public and private, were facing the same dilemma.

As the recession peaked after the first decade in the 2000s, higher education continued struggling financially. Students were protesting for a quality education that was affordable and worth the investment, while schools were scuttling to balance lack of funds with competitive learning opportunities. Classrooms were now over-crowded and faculty cutbacks were epidemic. Several colleges no longer had scholarship money to offer, and, for public institutions, when state funding ran out, classes were cancelled.[6]

At my university, students were leaving to pursue general education requirements and degrees at public and community colleges where the cost, though still on the rise, was more affordable. This, in turn, created jam-packed classrooms at those schools, impacting how effectively professors could instruct. A U.S. News article *The Great Recession's Toll on Higher Education* states that enrollment in schools that offered lower costs increased 16% in 2009, a significant jump.[7] Eventually night classes, as well as online courses, became available to cater to the influx of new students. Millennials were receptive to this, as we no longer placed emphasis on where or when our institutions offered courses, but instead on our own future financial stability.

Though Millennials transitioned to lower paying institutions, the cost to attend any college still rose faster than inflation. As noted by College Board trends, from

2009-10 to 2014-15, the tuition costs to attend a public four-year school increased by 17%, and for the same five-year time span, the costs to attend a private nonprofit four-year school rose by 10%. Since 1984-85, tuition rates have increased in public four-year schools by 225%, or an average of 4% each year over 30 years, and in private four-year schools by 146%, i.e. 3% per year over 30 years.[8] What is widening the gap of those who can afford an education and those who can't is that income is not increasing in sync with rising tuition rates, thus putting a strain on students and supportive family members who wish to provide financial support.

How has this affected graduates? Nicknamed the Boomerang Generation, Millennials have made our way back home after college graduation, applied for jobs our degrees could not help us with, and waited out the economy. Now as we enter the work world, we take on lower starting salaries.

Millennials across the board are experiencing "delayed adulthood." Our student loan lenders, however, remain persistent, and stop us from accomplishing things that Baby Boomers and Gen-Xers had the luxury of doing, like purchasing our first homes and starting families early on. Even affording to have a savings account is nearly impossible. According to the Wells Fargo Millennial study in 2014, 56% of Millennials reported living paycheck-to-paycheck, without the means to save for the future, and

47% of us use more than half of our monthly income to pay off debt.[9]

Those of us who want to avoid the process of paying now, choose to go back to school for a Master's degree, hoping to earn more industry-specific skills for a higher paying job. Others rely on income-based repayment, or IBD, backed by the government. This way we are only paying back what we can afford, which is a nice option, but not practical if wanting to pay off loans sooner rather than later.

IBD can extend loan re-payments, and, subsequently, the interest rates that go along with it. There is also the option of loan consolidation, but drawbacks might include losing loan forgiveness options, increased interest rates or inferior interest rate discounts, and the elimination of benefits like loan cancellation if you work in public service.[10] Lastly, there are those who just ignore their loans; the Federal Reserve Bank of New York noted that, for the last quarter of 2014, student loan delinquency rates reached 11.3%.[11]

What does this mean? Looking back, I ask myself several questions: 1) Was the education I received worth it? 2) How long will it take me to accomplish goals that will affect my future? 3) What pitfalls can subsequent generations avoid?

If I had been more prudent in my student loan research, I would have realized there is always leftover money and funds through independent scholarships, the cost of living on campus adds to the surmounting debt, and interest rates vary per loan type. I simply needed the money and needed it fast in order to meet class-enrollment deadlines, and did not invest time exploring better alternatives. Even paying off loans while still in school could have saved me thousands.

Now a Southern California resident after staying in town once graduating, I was able to secure employment and find an apartment. To make ends meet and afford to pay back $600 per month of student loans with my low-starting salary, I swap out unneeded wants like cable television for Netflix, avoid buying items, whether technology or groceries, at full price, and sell things that I no longer use regularly, including clothing and furniture. Colleagues rely on other methods of saving, such as not owning a car, dining in frequently, renting with a roommate, or opting to live at home with parents and family.

Even by saving, luxuries like owning a home undoubtedly fall to the backburner as the new goal becomes paying off debt. The American Dream for Millennials is not homeownership, but to get rid of student loans that keeps us financially at risk.[12] This becomes significant for this generation as we start to evaluate our future and what we realistically can afford, mortgages being one of the first things we nix.

Additionally, after living through the recession and housing crisis that affected our parents, we are more debt-averse and less likely to take on a 30-year mortgage. A U.S. Census Bureau report shares that 69.2% of Americans were homeowners in 2004, but, by the third quarter of 2014, only 64.4% of Americans owned homes; spotlighting that homeownership is declining as Millennials reach adulthood.[13] The New York Federal Reserve also reports a decline in homeownership, focusing in on 30-somethings, reporting that only 22% of people who had student loan debt owned a home in 2013, compared to 34% owning a home in 2008.[14]

What are the costs that come with owning a home that have Millennials looking the other way? In addition to the increase in monthly payments, compared to what we can pay in rent, purchasing property relies on having a significant down payment (even FHA loans have subsequent fees), as well as funds set aside in a savings account that will continue to mature over time. If you do rely on your savings for the down payment, you have to adequately explain how you plan on replenishing this in the future. And, most importantly, your debt-to-income ratio has to be around 43/57.[15] Factor in the cost of repairs, maintenance and upkeep (e.g. replacing a broken washer and dryer, maintaining yard work, covering HOA fees if applicable, etc) and owning a home can lead to additional financial stress. By taking into account costs and adding it to the debt Millennials already owe, homeownership is less of something that we need right now.

Despite the looming debt Millennials carry however, we are confident that we won't take our payments to the grave, something that Baby Boomers and Gen-Xers are concerned about with their own financials. A recent national survey by Credit-cards.com reveals that the age group 18-29, compared to others, believes they are least likely to be stuck with debt forever;[16] a silver lining for a generation that was not given too many opportunities for stability. Thus, even though Millennials do not have immediate access to funds, or employment with better starting wages to help us reach financial freedom, we are optimistic about our future. We've graduated to a type of adulthood where we shakily find ways to survive, while remaining confident that we can accomplish our new American Dream.

Five Things You Didn't Realize About Student Debt

1) **Many students underestimate how much debt they are taking on.** In December 2014, The Brookings Institute revealed that only 24% of students with federal loans were able to estimate within 10% of the actual value of their loan.[17]

2) **Debt consolidation and loan refinancing are not the same.** Debt consolidation is the process of taking multiple loans and combining them together as one. With help from the government, federal loans can only be consolidated with other federal loans. When consolidating federal loans, the new interest rate is calculated by taking the weighted average of the prior interest rates.

   For private loans, consolidation happens through a private lender. In regards to interest rates, instead of taking the weighted average of previously combined loans, a new rate is calculated, factoring in financial history and credit score. This, in essence, is loan refinancing.

Loan refinancing, similar to debt consolidation, involves combining multiple loans. However, a new interest rate is reformulated based on financial situation and credit score.

3) **Income-Based Repayment and Pay-As-You-Earn Repayment plans are not equal.** Income-Based Repayment (IBR) is one repayment option to help manage the weight of paying back federal student loans, including Stafford, Grad PLUS, or Consolidation loans. Payment caps are based on income and family size, with the amount owed annually equaling 15% of the difference between your adjusted gross income (AGI) and 150% of the federal poverty line. Typically, loan forgiveness occurs after 25 years. However, for new IBR borrowers who signed up on or after July 1, 2014, the repayment period is 20 years.

An initiative launched by Barack Obama in 2012, Pay As You Earn (PAYE) is another option for those with student loans to set up a repayment plan based on their current financial situation. Unlike Income-Based Repayment, you are only eligible if you did not owe money on a federal student loan as of October 1, 2007 *and* received a disbursement of a direct loan on or after

October 1, 2011. Additionally, PAYE repayments only work for federal direct loans.

Other things to note regarding Pay As You Earn: similar to IBR, monthly payments are calculated based on adjusted gross income. How much is owed annually equals 10% of the difference between your AGI and 150% of the Poverty Guideline for your family size, a 5% decrease in the cap proposed for Income-Based Repayment. Ultimately, with Pay As You Earn, your monthly payments will be lower compared to IBR.

PAYE's loan forgiveness occurs at 20 years, which, in some cases, is five years sooner than IBR and, in order to be eligible for PAYE and IBR, economic hardship must be determined.[18]

4) **You owe taxes on loan-forgiveness awards.** For student loan forgiveness awards given through a program like AmeriCorps, the amount applied to your loan that year is considered taxable income. Thus, depending on which tax bracket you fall into, you will owe a calculated amount.

5) **Co-signers are on the hook for student loan debt delinquency.** Parents or family members who co-sign for student loans are equally responsible for paying back the lender. As Tamara Krause shares online at eStudentLoan, if the party responsible for making monthly payments defaults, the co-signer is not only on the hook for the initial payment, but for accrued interest rates and fees. Additionally, credit score is negatively affected for both parties if payments are delinquent. Also keep in mind that when co-signing for a loan it is not as easy to discharge from the shared responsibility of the loan, unless the other party has proven themselves to be financially responsible by making timely monthly payments over a span of 12-24 months.[19]

4

Quarter Life Crisis

Truth Bomb:

After psychologist Oliver Robinson from the University of Greenwich in London and colleagues interviewed 50 participants age 25-35 years who have experienced a quarter life crisis, he broke down the phases that complete the lifecycle of the mid-life crisis' younger sibling:

1) The feeling of being trapped by life choices, including being stuck in a career or romantic relationship

2) Experiencing the "need to get out" of whatever is causing the sense of entrapment

3) Starting over and rebuilding your life

4) Establishing new commitments that are more in tune with your interests and aspirations

Eighty percent of participants who went through a quarter-life crisis cite that it was a positive experience. Millennials who reevaluate life priorities earlier on in order to revisit goals not being achieved, subsequently diminish the risks of going through a mid-life crisis.[1]

—

On the eve of my 25th birthday, I lay in bed, my studio apartment typically a space where I could find stillness and composure, though not tonight. My cat curled in the crook created by my rib cage. I was restless and fearful. Remembering my friends' experiences with their 25th birthday when I was 22, 23, and then 24 years old, I recalled convincing them that they were still young, left with a lot more to accomplish. I had become a proselytizer of age, brightly stating that, as we become older, personal growth ensues. Now it was my turn. The knot in my stomach that I had been ignoring all of my birthday month unfurled until it had taken up roots in my gut. I had made it to a quarter of a century, but I still couldn't figure out what I was doing to move forward and reach success.

Call it dramatic, but turning 25 is significant. I had been hit with the idea that I would not exist forever. Time was moving so quickly that my childhood dreams seemed to shrink as I grew bigger. Knees to chest, curled under covers, I verbalized to no one that I was afraid to lose. My career path, loneliness, and subsequent depression were getting to me. I was stuck in student loan debt, bored at work, and unable to find a match romantically.

Combined with those frustrations, I was compounded with decision after decision and life ultimatums: take on another job to deal with debt quicker versus draw out my monthly payments and live now; go back to school for a Master's degree or take a pay cut to jump into another career field that I would love more; move back home and save, or continue to live independently paycheck to paycheck. I was uncertain what I should do next, knowing that what I had envisioned accomplishing by this age would not be achieved. Now, what I ultimately feared was becoming complacent and stuck.

Research conducted by GumTree.com notes that 86% of young people feel pressured to fulfill their dreams by the age of 30.[2] However, as Millennials, we are confronted with economic burdens unlike those Baby Boomers and Gen-Xers faced. We are career-driven in a job market that continues to stall, and, although we may not want to settle down into marriage right now, finding a romantic partner who understands our career goals and can advocate for us is taxing. Dealing with these pressures as we transition into adulthood triggers what is now referred to as a quarter life crisis.

On that evening, the night I turned 25, midnight had struck. There were no church bells, just hymns of foot and car traffic, television from neighbors, and the occasional bass from passing vehicles making up the rhythm of Los Angeles. I had only to rely on the sanctity of my iPhone to alert me that I was now a quarter way through my life. I was halfway to fifty, as well as halfway through my twenties. This was really happening and, with fewer milestones left after college graduation, the faster life seemed to occur. Important events were not measured in compartmentalized timelines anymore. There were no four years here marking the completion of one phase of life, and then four years there indicating the ending of another. This contributed to a sense of feeling directionless, isolated, and depressed.

Multiple studies have spotlighted that Millennials experience depression at higher rates compared to Baby Boomers and Gen-Xers. When it comes to depression on the job, for example, Bensinger, DuPont, & Associates cite that one out of five Millennial employees sought their assistance for work-life help.[3]

One idea of why this could be indicates that Millennials feel trapped in a job role that's meaningless, unrelated to their talents, and that offers zero to no feedback or positive impact on their lives. The only stability amounts from a paycheck that helps pay back loans after attending and graduating college.

Another reason explains that a lot of Millennials grew up in sheltered environments, which included and still includes the involvement of parents in day-to-day decision-making. Shifting from a sheltered environment or a scenario where Millennials were accustomed to helicopter parenting puts us in a more fragile emotional state.[4] Living independently becomes an obstacle, when we're used to consulting with our parents frequently on how to resolve daily issues or have them fight our battles up to and throughout college and, in some occasions, at work. All of this creates a climate where we become more depressed and anxious. Now, especially, it is more common for 20-somethings to be considered not as adults, but trapped in a pre-adulthood stage, or what's been referred to as delayed adulthood.[5]

After my mid-20s breakdown on the eve of my birthday, I was not equipped for next steps in life. I wanted to travel, revisiting my study-abroad days in college, invest in others, and build a well-rounded life that involved my understanding society and other cultures. I valued fulfillment without a paycheck, but struggled knowing that a paycheck was the only way I could afford to keep myself financially afloat. My options felt scarce, and the opportunities I wanted to take advantage of didn't seem financially viable to pursue or within reach.

Though seemingly solitary, my conundrums at age 25 are widely experienced by other Gen-Yers. Alice Stapleton, Generation-Y and Quarter-Life Crisis expert, shares in her article *Under Pressure: As a Millennial experiencing the Quarter Life Crisis,* "The reality of the 9-5 is a sheer disappointment for many. Many of my coaching clients describe elation at getting their first job, to which they gave little thought, focusing heavily on the desperate need to earn following university, to pay off student and credit card loans. A couple of years later, the dust settles and they start to wake up and realize they have started down a path that does not suit them, their values, or priorities in life."[6]

Soon after my B-day blues, I was relieved when one of my co-workers detailed that he wanted to figure out a way to give back to society and live without the stressors of a 9-5 job position. All of this he shared while we carpooled to a client dinner. He longed to find himself outside of the office identity that interpolated between who he wanted to be and who he was becoming. I couldn't help thinking: are we living the dream or our worst nightmare?

Weighing Millennials' accomplishments against those of Baby Boomers and Generation Xers and what we have achieved by the age of 25 seems to be less. The American Dream of establishing ourselves as a homeowner with 2.5 children and a corporate career are not priorities of this generation's up and coming adults.

Instead, our main concern gives importance to taking care of debt. According to the 2014 Wells Fargo Millennial Study, out of the 1,600 Gen-Yers surveyed, 39% state they are overwhelmed by debt, compared to only 23%

of Baby Boomers, and a huge number of us financially aren't at a place to establish savings.[7] BuzzFeed writer Erin Chack even quips in her post *25 Signs You're Almost 25*, Millennials aren't even certain what an IRA is.[8] What could we really have accomplished in this short period of time, compared to preceding generations, with our unique limitations of unaffordable education, a sluggish job market, and being taught to be co-dependent, not self-reliant, due to helicopter parenting?

Right now, life seems confusing–as if I'd recently graduated college–and sometimes increasingly lonelier. The job that I imagined having did not meet my expectations, and finding a fulfilling career path is difficult in a competitive market with what seems to be few opportunities. Outside of work, my social life alternates between phases of exploring the latest music, fashions, and celebrity culture, or forgoing it all and finding solace in running errands. I fluctuate between going out at night or staying in, turning on Netflix, and eating ice cream for dinner.

When I do want to experience the night scene, I relish in the idea that I'm still in my 20s, and that I should take advantage of this while I can. Then I realize I am almost past the halfway mark to 30 after my hangovers seem more merciless. I am still struggling to make everything line up.

This isn't what I envisioned when I looked at my college acceptance letter, and was told I could do whatever I dreamed of if I worked for it persistently and feverishly. I had become the classic academic overachiever, constantly seeking approval and ways to make my efforts feel that much more special, when a different landscape was waiting for me after I graduated.

What can I really start to accomplish for others and myself? I'm not completely sure yet, but I'm confident that I will be soon as I continue to work out what means the most to me in life. I may not be able to "Eat-Pray-Love" my way out of this by quitting my job and embarking on a getaway around the world, but, as I come to terms with what I really want, what I can afford to accomplish, and who I want to share these exciting and equally trying moments with, I'm secure in knowing that, at this age, there are a lot of unknowns that I have yet to discover.

While I do not know everything, I'm closer to knowing who I am. So, although everything still feels incredibly out of place and messy, I begrudgingly remember that I'm still only a quarter way through, and things will snap to if I continue to question where I want to land in life and then follow through with the goals I set into motion.

Five Very Real Struggles Millennials Face During a Quarter Life Crisis:

1. **Going Back to School:** Should we get an MBA to better our chances in the career pool, or will we only be taking on more debt, potentially sacrificing job experience for a higher level of education? Maybe we can study in Germany or one of the Nordic countries that allows Americans to pursue a degree with little to no costs.

   Will we continue to be overeducated and underemployed, or will niche skills improve our opportunities to be successful and fulfilled at a job where we have an optimal chance to explore our passion and talents? All of the above are normal quandaries Millennials take on when considering the risk-reward system of higher education.

2. **To Travel or Not Travel:** In the savvy words of *All Groan Up* author Paul Angone, "You're 99.7% sure a road trip would fix everything."[9] Revisiting the culture, the sense of adventure and empowerment, as well as the ability to learn about ourselves experienced during our college study abroad trip or a time when we were able to leave home and get away, seems like a quick and easy

fix. Becoming a yoga instructor, taking a meditative workshop where we're doing juice cleanses on a beach, or horseback riding in Nicaragua, are options we try to convince ourselves we need to recalibrate. Can we afford to satisfy our taste for wanderlust, or just plunge into more debt and figure out the specifics later?

3. **Shrinking Our Inner Circle:** Sometimes we just need to cut out friends who aren't bringing that much value to the table. We're done with the drama, he-said/she-said feuds, the lengthy monologues of excuses and explanations over Facebook chat, and the overall fear that this person isn't truly in our corner. Now we just keep it simple and aim for friendships that improve who we are instead of dragging us down. We're recognizing that the quality of friends is more important than how many friends we have in our inner circle, and Millennials are cleaning house.

4. **Finding the Right Job:** We've had more job changes since graduating than the amount of toppings options at our favorite froyo spot. Does our résumé look like we're job-hopping? Probably, but it's all in the quest to find a fulfilling career path. Once we jump into a role, we realize it feels meaningless and unproductive, so we're lured into the next position that offers perks like

ping-pong in a break room, free lunches (though I'm pretty sure there's no such thing in economics), and unlimited vacation days, only to realize this job is just as soul-crushing as the last. Where do we want to land? The job hunt continues.

5. **Marriage and Kids:** As the Internet meme goes, half of our friends are married with kids and the other half are drunk and can't find their phones. Why does it feel like everyone is settling down, while we're just figuring out how to keep one foot in front of the other, financially and career wise. We can barely afford the responsibility of taking care of a dog, let alone a tiny human. Plus, being invited to participate in one more wedding is going to deplete what little savings we do have.

5

Check Your Privilege

Truth Bomb:

The "Missing White Woman Syndrome" phenomenon is a way to describe media coverage that isolates and focuses on stories of missing upper class White youth and adults, compared to the societal disinterest of missing Black and/or poor community members. Is this one example of "White privilege?" Absolutely.[1]

—

I returned home from a friend's hipster-style birthday bash at a swanky outdoor restaurant. There were a few memorable things about this hidden, jungle-landscaped space plopped in trendy Silverlake, Los Angeles, the not-so-great service being one of them. I left around midnight, angered about the wait staff, and annoyed that I would not be able to find parking in my permit zone when I returned home.

As I walked back to my apartment, I heard the trickling of water from an outdoor fountain in the backdrop. The spattered waterfalls drew my attention to my current living situation. I was walking from a party in a well-to-do neighborhood, wearing attire not regulated by the government, and experiencing the freedom to live on my own as a woman. This conscious run-on of thoughts continued until I reached the doorstep of my apartment, returning to the fountain of water and the observation that, in this neighborhood, we have water to use simply for decoration. Here, I was checking my privilege.

Social media has specifically targeted what's known as White privilege, a bias that absolutely should be acknowledged. Violence against innocent, unarmed Black Americans by White American civilians and law enforcement has generated significant media attention. Wealth gaps between minorities and White Americans have not diminished. And disproportionate unemployment rates, as well as uneven educational infrastructures still continue to create an unfair playing field for people of color. It's fair to say that race and ethnicity are pre-cursors that often affect quality of living, leaving Black Americans and people of color underprivileged in plenty of societal and economic spaces. However, backlash still suggests that

"White privilege" does not exist even in light of the "Check Your Privilege" sentiment.

Tal Fortgang's divisive article "Checking My Privilege: Character as The Basis of Privilege" first published in *The Princeton Tory*[2] attempts to discredit the notion of racial bias. Fortgang theorizes that one's success is simply based on a matter of merit. He fails to acknowledge the experiences of those who are non-White, and also non-male, a privilege in and of itself. Fortgang also does this while exercising his privilege to voice concerns and have his thoughts picked up by an international publication.

In contrast to Fortgang's views, race is a characteristic that has a profound effect on how we treat people. For centuries, "White" has been understood as the standard. Diversified media representation, while steadily improving in film, though not in sitcom television, continues to feature White Americans. White males chiefly dominate jobs behind the scenes in the entertainment industry with 94% of film studio heads being White and 100% being male.[3]

This means messaging and core values of one group are expressly indoctrinated into American culture repeatedly, while mainly caricatured views of underrepresented groups are fed into society. To have someone's culture largely distorted by another community is a major disadvantage to people of color that can lead to racial bias for minorities, while being a privilege to those who are White.

Media representation is one instance of many that touches on racial privilege, but perhaps the most interesting that Millennials of all races are drawing attention to is that skin color can be a determining factor for a snap judgment life or death sentence.

As expert storyteller Malcolm Gladwell relays in his bestseller *Blink,* society has learned to unconsciously associate "white with good" as this type of cultural messaging surrounds us everyday. Gladwell points this out in reference to taking the Race Implicit Association Test (IAT) exam, which measures the unconscious attitudes of people toward White and Black races, as well as predicts what our behavior may be in a spontaneous moment. As noted in *Blink,* it's common for people, including minorities, to have a stronger positive association with people who are White.[4]

This bias can be especially dangerous when minorities are face-to-face with law enforcement. Observing data from 2015 alone, unarmed Black Americans are twice as likely to be killed compared to White or Hispanic counterparts.[5]

Comedian Louis CK recognizes this and his inherent privilege in a memorable stand-up performance stating, "Let me be clear, by the way. I'm not saying that

White people are better. I'm saying that being White is clearly better. Who could even argue? If it was an option, I would re-up every year. 'Oh, yeah, I'll take 'White' again, absolutely. I've been enjoying that. I'm gonna stick with White, thank you.'"[6]

How deep does our love for fair skin go? Observing how the "Missing White Woman Syndrome" can affect modern-day missing persons cases, another organization revealed something else regarding race and the general population's level of empathy.

A story launched where a blonde Norwegian pre-teen girl named Thea was set to marry a 37-year-old in a child-bride scenario. Details of the upcoming nuptials, including nerves, wedding gown pictures, and parental involvement were shared on the tween's blog. The story generated copious amounts of press, and law enforcement was even contacted.

The child-bride scenario turned out to be a hoax and ultimately a campaign by Plan Norway to bring awareness to the statistic that 1 out of 9 girls worldwide are married off before they reach age 15.[7] A White face was used to stimulate discussion about problems that largely affect minority children, as Whiteness is what we are socialized to care about. In African, Indian, and Asian cultures, where minorities are aware of this racial bias, skin-lightening creams have cropped up, marketed mainly to women who are certain that with fair skin comes a better chance of receiving basic human rights.

Despite Fortgang's beliefs in a system set up to award others on merit alone, biases of many kinds outside of race also exist and it's important that we acknowledge a few of them. Many people, including non-males, members of the LGBT+ community, those who aren't Christian, or even people with a mental or physical disorder experience biases daily. On the flip side, people who are heterosexual and cisgender, Christian, and able-bodied benefit from those biases. It only takes being aware of these differences to shape how we interact with others. Acknowledging these privileges is a difficult task though.

Choosing to disregard our privileges may be easier than awareness, either because we are unable to articulate the advantages that we have, or we do not want to believe that, in some instances, we benefited from socialized biases and not merit alone. More and more Millennials are starting to point out the privileges we often ignore however, recognizing how we can oftentimes unconsciously contribute to inequalities. Essentially, we're encouraging others and ourselves to "check our privilege."

As an American, I was born into a nation and culture where I have human rights. Since the beginning of American culture, these rights have evolved for women and minorities in particular, where we now have access to higher education and employment, the right to vote, as well as the liberty to support ourselves independently. And, for women, when the time comes, we are able to marry a partner of our choosing.

As a woman in America, I feel safe to publically decry institutions that do not support an agenda for gender equality. I know that by doing this, an acid attack will not follow due to my verbalizations, my family members and I will not be a target for merciless violence by community members or ruling governance, and that younger family members who are girls can go to school without fear of bombings or being kidnapped.

These privileges that I possess, foremost as an American, are not accessible to all in developing countries. Across the globe, women are confronted by men daily (and their male privilege) who ban them from learning institutions, physically mutilate them when they rebel against liberties such a marriage, and force girls into submissive roles through constant sexual abuse and motherhood. As of 2011, statistics showed that 603 million women were inhabitants of countries where domestic violence was not considered a crime.[8]

When I hear women proclaim anti-feminist rhetoric in order to uphold traditional men-women gender roles in America, I have to remind them to check their privilege. In Western culture specifically, having the luxury to denounce something publically, as a woman, without penalty of death, is a privilege. I too have to remember to check my privilege, knowing that the right to fight for gender equality should be accessible to all.

Other privileges often overlooked include those that come with being heterosexual or cisgender. Establishing LGBT+ rights is essential, and this generation is making seismic shifts to ensure everyone regardless of sexual orientation or gender identity, experiences equality. Being heterosexual, as well as cisgender, comes with some ostensible privileges, however, regardless of the fair rights we strive to pursue.

The ability to share public displays of affection, not having derogatory slang created to describe who we are ubiquitous in common conversations (i.e., phrasing such as "that's gay," "faggot," or "lesbo," among others), learning in a safe educational environment as an adolescent, or having an accessible public restroom are a few examples of heterosexual and cisgender privilege.

People who are heterosexual or cisgender get a free pass to experience quotidian events absent of verbal or physical assault. Think of the increased suicide rates and homelessness prevalent among LGBT+ youth, torn families, and misguided hate by way of some political, as well as religious, organizations. By acknowledging privileges and freedoms we benefit from, we can extend them to those who lack the advantages that we have.

Western American culture is a one-nation-under-God society, where utmost value is placed on Christianity. Christian privilege is so intertwined with our culture that politics, learning institutions, and businesses all, at some point, facilitate Christian practice. One example includes that as Christians, we are absolutely certain we will receive time off from school and work, without penalty, for celebration of our beliefs. Also, we are confident that we can find décor, as well as paraphernalia and materials to invest in, in order to participate in worship. And finally, as we partake in Christian holidays, we can be confident that our greetings are known and understood, even by those who are not affiliated with our religious teachings, a privilege that those who are not Christian do not have. We don't immediately recognize these biases, as they oftentimes have zero impact on our lives, until something catastrophic occurs that draws our attention to it.

After the September 2001 attacks, for example, those who shared Islamic views experienced hate crimes, harassment, and violence from citizens. The November 2015 terrorist attacks in Paris from extremist group Islamic State of Iraq and the Levant (ISIL) also furthered the miscategorization of Islam as a hateful and violent religion.

Six-time NBA champion Kareem Abdul-Jabbar spoke out about religious misconceptions following the Charlie Hebdo January Paris attack. He appropriately summed up Christian privilege, stating, "When the Ku

Klux Klan burn a cross in a black family's yard, prominent Christians aren't required to explain how these aren't really Christian acts. Most people already realize that the KKK doesn't represent Christian teachings. That's what I and other Muslims long for—the day when these terrorists praising the Prophet Muhammad or Allah's name as they debase their actual teachings are instantly recognized as thugs disguising themselves as Muslims."[9]

Though these acts of terrorism have bastardized Islamic views, members of Islam were and still are subject to prejudices. Conversely, hate groups in America who commit crimes in the name of Christianity are not viewed as terrorism. They are ultimately seen for what they are: not as acts of Christianity, but as a gross misrepresentation of Christian beliefs.

Among the privileges Millennials are remembering to check, being an able-bodied citizen is one we might overlook. Disabled Americans, including those with physical, learning, and mental challenges, face discriminatory battles daily. Even with my mental disorder as a person battling depression, I know I am more likely to face stigma and discrimination.

Considered the largest minority group worldwide, those who are disabled typically suffer from economic hardship. This is a combined result of not being able to secure employment and the necessity to cover medical costs. As this minority group is less likely to find sufficient employment, it is not uncommon for those with a disability to live below the poverty line. Observing U.S. Census Data, individuals age 15-64 living with a disability experienced a poverty rate of approximately 28.6% in 2010, while those without disability experienced a poverty rate of 14.3%, a mind-numbing disparity.[10]

In regards to mental health, the poorer you are, the more likely you will be set up to fail. Expertly explained in Liz Szabo's *USA Today* piece *Cost of Not Caring: Stigma Set in Stone*, she reveals, "States cut $5 billion from mental health services from 2009 to 2012, along with 10% of psychiatric hospital beds."[11] Discounting mental disorders as illnesses that can actually be treated results in cut funding and increased stigma. This type of discrimination alone leaves many without financial options to seek treatment, as well as the fear to seek treatment at all.

Here's a quick exercise: imagine what a "normal" body looks like. What are some characteristics you envision? A person capable of walking and moving without aid, the ability to hear, see, and fully experience the world with all our of senses, the capacity to understand minute details in body language, or rhythmic complexities like processing and creating memories using our mental faculties. Maybe you simply picture someone dexterous enough to walk up a flight of stairs, carry groceries, drive a car, or use the bathroom independently.

The above descriptions apply to those considered able-bodied. Often our first thought when we think of a "normal" person reflects a body type that's fully capable of functioning physically and mentally. We have been taught that bodies with physical differences, or people with mental or learning disabilities, are inferior. They are frequently excluded from participating with people who are "normal."

Those who are able-bodied take advantage of privileges such as enjoying group activity inclusion, from recreational sports participation to travelling with ease. We are also well represented in the media: our role models, superheroes, and inspirational fictional characters are certain to be able-bodied. In addition, we know our ability will not be used as a punch line in television shows or movies.

Only a few contemporary television shows, including *Glee*, are credited for cast diversity in relationship to body-ability diversity. Wheelchair-bound character Artie Abrams, played by Kevin Mchale, and Becky Jackson, a student living with Down syndrome, played by Lauren Potter, both had recurring feature roles on the hit television show.

Realizing the privileges that I have is difficult, because I want to believe I accomplished everything with sheer talent, merit, and hard work, not the advantages that I was born into. Yet recognizing what I benefit from is not a means to devalue what I have succeeded at doing. Instead, it's knowing that the faulty belief that everyone exists on equal footing only alienates society from accelerating progress and achieving equality.

Millennials recognize that the goal is not to help minorities attain success by simply providing a platform, but to recreate normalizations where the majority-minority polarity does not exist. In order to do this, we have to be cognizant of the advantages we have and remember to routinely check our privilege.

Here are 10 Questions We Can Ask to Check Our Privilege Regularly

1) What describes a "first world problem" (e.g., Netflix not functioning correctly, your favorite flavor of froyo not being available, or in my case, not receiving adequate service at a restaurant)?

2) Are you career impaired or likely to experience discrimination against landing employment based on race, gender, sexuality, or health?

3) Has there ever been an occasion where you were forced to live without food?

4) Name a time period where you've had to lie about your sexuality in order to avoid harassment or discrimination.

5) Do you feel safe publically displaying affection with a partner?

6) Have you ever been profiled, threatened, or ostracized for your religious beliefs?

7) Have you ever been called a name that is a racial slur?

8) Have you ever been questioned by law enforcement or other authority figures for being able to afford expensive luxury items?

9) Are you able to afford and/or have access to healthcare when needed?

10) Name a time when you experienced homelessness due to your gender or sexual identity.

6

I Can't Stand the Rain

Truth Bomb:

Examining data from the National Survey on Drug Use and Health, in 2014 there were an estimated 9.8 million adults 18 and up in the U.S. with a serious mental illness (SMI) including schizophrenia, paranoid and psychotic disorders, bipolar disorder, major depressive disorders and others. This is not to be confused with disorders categorized as non-serious, like forms of anxiety, phobias, PTSD, and some personality disorders.[1]

If you need immediate support or intervention, call the National Suicide Prevention Lifeline at 1-800-273-8255 or visit their website. Trained specialists are available 24/7.

———

  It was noon. Footsteps creaked past my studio apartment, neighbors bustling by to accomplish Saturday errands. I was hesitant to sit up, put on my best face, and get going with the usual routine of weekend responsibilities: cleaning, groceries, coffee dates. Instead, I checked my phone applications, looking for an easy out to "connect" with the living world. Awakening Facebook first, I eyed several new notifications that weren't there last night, and scanned through "likes" and comments on my latest musings: nothing socially relevant, just a casual post about my cat.

When I put my phone down, I tried to see beyond the darkness in my apartment, the various shades of dimming black becoming watery grays to my adjusting pupils. My depression was lulling me back into a state where I wanted to sleep, so I stayed in bed for the rest of the afternoon, adjusting the blinds to stop any julienned light from entering.

Contemporary society feels a particular uneasiness discussing mental health, creating a landscape where these conversations remain glacial. Ubiquitous among mental disorders is major depression. Regarded as the most common mental disorder in the United States, depression affects more than 16 million Americans each year.[2] Many of us move along in silence, not addressing what we experience, or acknowledging the suffering that friends and family members go through due to stigma. The misrepresentation that accompanies mental illness prevents us from recognizing it before it can consume us.

I knew from the moment I was diagnosed at 13 that having depression would be a quiet battle. While surviving adolescence and my late teens, I felt stuck and seemingly distant from my peers. From revolving diets that included multiple shifts in medication, bullying from colleagues who could sense that something was off, the struggle to find a therapist who understood me and what I needed, and ultimately a suicide attempt, I was so close to becoming a number, to contributing to the grim statistic of suicide being the third leading cause of death in the world for 15-44 year olds.[3] Though my experience was surprisingly common, I did not realize that I had the option to seek support groups and counseling, and connect with a community of others in a safe environment. I didn't realize this was an option, because no one was talking about it, though a lot of people may have been going through it themselves.

The fear of facing isolation and stigma prolongs our decision to disclose what we're going through, find effective treatment, and reach a place of contentment and safety. Collectively, people are reminded of the mental collapses and the extent to which a person has reached their breaking point when public shootings occur, the number of which has tripled since 2011 and sadly includes 74 school massacres to date.[4] Adolescent suicides are another indicator of the silence kept bottled in, and with my experience I can completely understand. But mental disorders aren't solely limited to teens and under.

Millennials are now part of the emerging 18-and-up age group where coping with depression as well as other mental disorders like anxiety, bipolar disorder, schizophrenia, eating disorders, or self-mutilation is more frequent. Our stressors, including unemployment or underemployment, finances, and living at home throughout our early adulthood are situations that are thought to contribute to what we are experiencing mentally.

A 2012 survey conducted by the American Psychological Association shared that 19% of Millennials have been told they have depression, compared to 14% of Gen-Xers and 11% of Baby Boomers.[5] We can't be sure if increased depression diagnoses correlate with the different stressors Millennials face, or if the prevalence of depression has actually increased. Additionally, preceding generations may not have been prone to reveal mental health concerns, also affecting the results of those surveyed. What we are aware of is that more Millennials receive some sort of mental health diagnosis. While Gen-Y learns to open up about our experiences with mental health, those of us who do feel comfortable sharing do so bravely and vulnerably.

Stand-up comedian Kevin Breel is one Gen-Yer, who, through his TED Talk *Confessions of a Depressed Comic*,[6] candidly expressed what it is like to live with depression. He prolifically states "Real depression is being sad when everything in your life is going right," clearly sharing his experience in a way that others can understand. His story went viral for the poignant details he addresses, as well as the profound clarity with which he speaks about his mental illness.

Another video that addresses mental health challenges is *Mental Health, It's Time to Talk*. The 10-minute short published on YouTube in 2012 and on content sharing site UpWorthy in 2014, relies on several candid confessions from Millennials to iterate how prevalent mental disorders are.

Created by Leeds University Union in UK, nine college students were filmed speaking about their mental disorders. Diagnoses include depression, eating disorders, obsessive-compulsive disorder (OCD), and Post Traumatic Stress Disorder (PTSD). Each story is woven together with the narrative that even though these students deal with a mental disorder, often characterized as taboo, they're truly not alone in their experiences.[7]

As more content like this is created and shared across the Web, more people are compelled to share their story. Even celebrities like Lady Gaga and Demi Lovato have come forward admitting that they struggle with mental illness whether it's with depression as is the case with Gaga, or bulimia, self-harm, and drug abuse which Lovato battled.

During what seemed like the lowest part of my life, I felt alone and isolated. School administration didn't understand what was happening, my family was scared, and my friends became exhausted with my behavior. It wasn't until I was placed in group therapy that I realized I was not alone.

Every day for several months I would meet in a medium-sized room with patients of all sorts to verbally work through life traumas. There was a sense of relief when sharing my story. And, as it happens my story had commonalities with the stories of others: we all in some ways felt trapped, invisible, and out of control. We were only able to realize how much we had in common by being there together.

Developing trust and a relationship with everyone in the room took patience. We vocalized our weaknesses to strip them little by little of their power. But most importantly, we listened. We were able to learn from others, including new, as well as healthy coping strategies. We also felt motivated to keep going with our treatment to get better. Talking about mental illness destigmatized it and made treatment much more smoother and effective.

Now that we have more insight on mental health issues, we can ask what's changing and what isn't. Examining and ultimately comparing celebrity experiences, such as the late comedian Robin Williams to that of actress Amanda Bynes, can give us more room to question the split ideals and feelings when looking at mental illness.

Picking up a tabloid featuring Amanda Bynes on the cover who was slumped over on a mall bench, I joked to a close friend how Bynes was becoming a typical child star wreck. That friend didn't laugh. Her frustrated sigh caught me off guard. She quickly recovered from her moment of anger and went on to patiently explain that Amanda Bynes was battling a mental illness, and that's not something we should make fun of. She concluded her slap-on-the-wrist response by asking why is it OK that we empathize with Robin Williams but bully Bynes?

Iconic funnyman, Robin Williams represented childlike lightheartedness. But because of his enigmatic personality, the general population didn't know about his fight with depression and anxiety until he took his life in August 2014. The passing of Robin Williams brought everyone together, iterating that more support is needed to educate others on what it means to have a mental illness.

Actress Amanda Bynes on the other hand was consistently featured in news sites for her left-of-center behavior believed to be triggered by bipolar disorder. Bynes' ups and downs occurred during the same timeline of Robin Williams' death. However, her behavior triggered the opposite effect of public empathy, drawing ridicule instead.

The extreme difference in how both celebrities were treated by the public shows how varied our feelings and perceptions are on mental illness. In reality, however, with so many people struggling, this shouldn't be the case. We should all be united to confront the stigma regardless of who is suffering or what a person is suffering from.

Looking at the numbers across generations, very few people are alone when dealing with a mental illness. The World Health Organization (WHO), for example, reported that, in 2012, 350 million people globally suffered from depression, and the mental disorder has been categorized as common.[8] Additional statistics from the Anxiety and Depression Association of America (ADAA) show anxiety disorders impacted 40 million Americans age 18 and older, costing the U.S. $42 billion a year to treat.[i] For bipolar disorder, 5.5 million Americans age 18 and up suffered.[9]

Though Millennials are savvy at navigating conversations on social justice and political issues, we're learning how to discuss mental health, as we now know it affects so many of us. We're also figuring out how to articulate what we're experiencing. The more we continue to inform ourselves on the subject and open up about our own battles, the more we can demystify what mental illness really is and the more we can come to realize that we are not alone even when it feels like we're the only ones standing in the rain.

Common Mental Illnesses and Myths

1) Anxiety Disorder–**Myth:** People who claim to have an anxiety disorder really just worry a lot or are neurotic, and nothing can help them. **Truth:** Therapy and medication can help stabilize a person suffering from an anxiety disorder. A person with an anxiety disorder should not be written off as neurotic and, instead, adequately supported in seeking treatment.[10]

2) Attention Deficit Hyperactivity Disorder (ADHD)–**Myth:** ADHD only affects boys. **Truth:** Girls are just as likely to struggle with ADHD, but may not be diagnosed until much later. Psychotherapist and coach Terry Matlen expertly notes that they "are more likely to be daydreaming, staring out the window, twisting their hair." Their symptoms are more difficult to spot and thus girls aren't as easily diagnosed as boys.[11]

3) Autism Spectrum Disorder–**Myth:** Autism Spectrum Disorder affects few. **Truth:** According to Centers for Disease Control and Prevention, about 1

in 68 children have been identified with Autism Spectrum Disorder.[12]

4) Bipolar Disorder–**Myth:** People suffering from bipolar disorder shift from mania to depressive states quickly. **Truth:** The experience of each person differs. Some may linger in depressive states for much longer. The experience is not consistent across all people diagnosed.[13]

5) Borderline Personality Disorder (BPD)–**Myth:** BPD only affects women. **Truth:** Research indicates that, although frequent amongst women, borderline personality disorder can affect men as well, and is fairly common.[14]

6) Depression–**Myth:** If diagnosed with depression, you will always be dependent on medication. **Truth:** Medication therapy varies from person-to-person, and sometimes has no effect at all, meaning that antidepressants are not an effective treatment option for everyone.[15]

7) Eating Disorders–**Myth:** Eating disorders are all about food. **Truth:** Under- or over-indulging in

food is just a symptom of the eating disorder used to block or suppress painful thoughts or emotions.[16]

8) Obsessive-Compulsive Disorder (OCD)–**Myth:** People who are neat freaks must have OCD. **Truth:** Cleanliness and OCD are not exclusively linked. People who like to clean or tidy up simply express cleanliness as a physical trait, which can be controlled at the will of that person. OCD, however, can manifest in hoarding, repetitive behaviors, or obsession over something bad happening.[17]

9) Panic Disorder–**Myth:** When having a panic disorder, you are likely to faint. **Truth:** While fainting is rare, other symptoms often include hyperventilation or shallow breath, as well as dizziness.[18]

10) Post-Traumatic Stress Disorder (PTSD)–**Myth:** People develop PTSD immediately after a traumatic event. **Truth:** Though PTSD symptoms typically occur within 3 months of the traumatic event, they can also take years to surface, subsiding and occurring later in life.[19]

11) Schizophrenia–**Myth:** People with schizophrenia have multiple personalities. **Truth:** Schizophrenia differs from split personality disorder. Those who suffer from schizophrenia experience delusions, false realities, at times hallucinations, in addition to other symptoms.[20]

7

All In A Day's Work

Truth Bomb:

Acknowledging that Millennials are experiencing a very different labor market is important to understanding why workplace behaviors are shifting for this generation. As the workplace climate continues to transform, the biggest challenge is dealing with multiple generations in the workplace at the same time. Millennials, in particular, require different training strategies and motivators. This can be difficult for companies and hiring managers to adapt to, but is necessary in order for organizations to evolve.

—

Millennials and Company Loyalty

I remember my college thesis being peppered with remarks like "'Do what you love" is as important as 'Putting food on the table,'" and "I will avoid taking a job that requires me to be hopped up on caffeine, only to later rely on sleeping pills to shut out anxieties." Later I discovered a lot of Millennials felt this way too, especially after graduating. Now, as we make up the majority of the workforce, we continue our search for meaningful roles in a field we're passionate about and that drives positive change.

An open loft-style space with pops of color, faux cabin furniture, and glass wall dividers that allowed for mapping out business plans with markers fit the bill to attract Millennials like myself. This was the first company I decided to work for full-time, and it was nothing like I had expected. Free of cubicles, stark colors, fluorescent lighting, and employees dressed in drab business attire, I was greeted by modern décor and a youthful energy. Perks included couches to nap on, unlimited snacks, and a stipend for monthly departmental bonding. To top it off, my job title as a writer was what I was looking for to launch my career.

Two months into the job, however, I discovered that these perks were the only things that the role had to offer. The CEO was an elusive figure, vacation days were limited, with some employees having to work over holidays, and the work I was doing never progressed further than copy-paste data entry. All of this equaled a position where there was little room for growth as a "writer" within the company.

As I had recently started the job role, however, I decided to stay for at least a year, despite the lack of meaningful work and professional growth. That's what other employees were doing. They explained the "writer" title at a reputable brand would be attractive on my résumé, and would help me negotiate for a higher starting salary later. Thinking of my student loans first, I decided that this was a smart idea. This was something I did not want to overlook in the short-term, but I knew I wasn't married to this position for the long-term. In order to land a fulfilling career, I would have to eventually jump ship, staying just long enough to give my résumé credibility.

Lydia Frank, editorial director at PayScale, echoes this sentiment impeccably in the 2014 *3rd Annual Study on the State of Gen Y Gen X and Baby Boomer Workers*, stating, "While it's easy to assume Millennials are willing to job-hop because they're less loyal to their employers than previous generations, you have to really look at the current economic climate to understand why that attitude has shifted over time. Millennials are often facing higher rates of underemployment, not to mention higher student loan debts, and they're struggling financially when they first enter the job market, so their first job might not be the one they were hoping for."[1]

Statistically speaking, job-hopping from one opportunity to a better one is common for Millennials. Fifty-eight percent of Gen-Yers surveyed by Upwork, formerly known as oDesk, reported that they expected to stay in their role for fewer than three years.[2] Despite the abundance of perks a company may offer, common motivators for succeeding on the job include having meaningful work and growth in the company. Millennials want projects that are both exciting and present us with an opportunity to advance. However, this may not be the case with current job roles, leaving us to languish in a position that doesn't progress our career goals and, in turn, may not be stable.

Labor economist Todd Sorensen digs into this further, skillfully demonstrating how the recession factors into Millennials' mindset of wanting career growth and ultimately steadiness. Using data from the IPUMS-USA database, he notes, "Millennials born in 1982, compared to those born in 1988, experienced very different labor markets early in their careers: the '82 Millennials were already 25 in 2007, before the start of the financial crisis. Others were only 20 years old when the financial crisis happened, and, thus, have never experienced a truly strong U.S. labor market."[3]

Looking at the numbers, a large segment of Generation-Y was forced to start careers in a volatile economy. As a result, Millennials are now searching for stability in jobs. Companies that have career advancement opportunities can provide this and retain Generation-Y talent, diminishing attrition rates and so-called disloyalty. Without career growth, however, Millennials realize it may take longer to become economically independent. That fact alone encourages this generation to move away from dead-end positions, and onward to other job roles that will lead to autonomy and stability.

Things Millennials Want Besides Perks

I. Team Bonding, Not Just Team Building

The Bureau of Labor reports that, as of 2015, Millennials make up the largest part of the U.S. workforce. However, the incompatible work styles of Generation-Y with Baby Boomers and Generation X have resulted in a labor market flooded with open jobs, but no potential hires. According to the same Bureau of Labor report, a staggering 4.8 million job openings existed in 2014; the highest number since January 2011.[4] As Gen-X and Baby Boomer leaders have hesitated to hire Millennial candidates, with 53% of managers reporting having difficulty hiring Millennials, and 39% of Millennials finding it challenging to land a traditional job, the labor force has remained unpredictable and, for some Gen-Yers, glum.[5]

What drives the uncertainty to hire Millennials rests in the differences of culture and values between Gen-Y and prior generations. Key divergences include office space and culture, outdated structures, as well as policies that Boomers and Xers enforce, and the adaptation of evolved technology. Arguably, Generation-Y was raised with an entrepreneurial spirit, learning how to invest in work we're passionate about, take advantage of technology at our fingertips, celebrate camaraderie and peer-to-peer teamwork, and break past traditions that simply aren't working anymore. We entered the workforce, expecting big business to share our work philosophies and values, but, in a lot of cases, they did not. These divergences produce breakdowns in communication.

Beginning with office space and culture, Millennials do enjoy a competitive workspace similar to prior generations. However, creating an atmosphere of success for everyone on the team is also valued. One way the culture at work can establish a feeling of teamwork is by cultivating ways for team members to bond, not only on the job, but outside of the office as well, something that Millennials relish.

Whereas Baby Boomers and Generation X may be tentative to mix professional and social lives, Millennials are all about it. Generation-Y thrives in this type of space, pioneering team bonding, instead of solely team building. Team building creates an atmosphere that teaches colleagues to work together as a cohesive unit to complete work-related projects; bonding creates an atmosphere that integrates socialization outside of team projects, along with developing the skills and trust to successfully complete an on-the-job task. Bonding captures the entire picture of interaction between peers.

After leaving my first out-of-college position in the spring of 2013, I ended up in a different job and, ultimately, different career by fall. My position as a writer stalled, and the market was calling for candidates eager to learn search engine optimization (SEO). I had minimal knowledge of SEO, but was up for a challenge, as it also tied into learning how to get more eyeballs on my online content. I applied for entry-level work in the digital marketing sphere. Taking the career jump was exciting, and the pay was enough to get me out of my parents' home in Orange County to a small studio apartment in Los Angeles. I could now afford to scrape by, versus not being able to survive on my own at all, and, to me, that was a small victory.

What was attractive about the digital marketing firm that went on to hire me was the company culture. According to a 2014 Glassdoor survey, company culture is ranked as one of the top five things job-searchers take into account before accepting an offer.[6] When I first walked into the office for the in-person interview, colleagues who were similar in age to me filled the vibrant, open-loft-style space. The office was punched up with bright red walls, original artwork and murals, as well as contemporary furniture. A high-backed chair that encased whoever was seated in it was the focal point of the lobby, along with a streamlined white couch. Bowls of candy and snack jars peppered the scenery, and denim-clad C-level execs sporting plaid button-downs and loafers rushed by, the front desk assistant excitedly pointing them out to me. Already the environment boasted an atmosphere of being up-to-date, modernized, fresh, and creative.

The front desk assistant shared fun facts about the company, including that the C-execs had desks on the floor to be easily accessible to employees. No one had an office, except for the human resources team. This was needed to maintain the privacy of employees, and make it easier for anyone to feel comfortable taking complaints to HR if a disturbance occurred. I immediately felt at home, a word that office spaces are using more and more to describe the at-work atmosphere. Another phrase organizations are using to paint a picture of company culture is "we're like a family." This company created that tight-knight bond from the beginning. Being hired by an organization that cared about their workers as individuals, and not just as warm bodies, was a relief.

Departmental stipends are important for this reason, and coincide with promoting a strong company culture. They allow co-workers to connect. Getting to know each other during fun events or outings away from the office creates a space where Gen-Yers can easily learn more about the people we're working with. Having this bonding time is essential to putting together a team that can trust and rely on each other. What this also establishes is transparency. Generation-Y wants to know if our team members are, in essence, good people. Overall, this can help with cross-team functionality, communication skills, and peer-to-peer learning, ultimately preparing Millennial workers to occupy spots in leadership roles.

On my very first day of working with this search engine optimization firm, I was assigned a "forced friend," a colleague to show me the ropes. We were given a budget once a month for three months to hang out outside of the office and get to know each other on a personal level. Activities included going to the movies, enjoying dinner, or even going out for yogurt. This peer was there so I could learn about the company and ask questions that I would normally be too intimidated to inquire about, and she could get to know me better as a team member. The pairing was a win-win-win that benefited the company in making sure they hired a great candidate, co-workers to ensure their new team member would mesh well with the group, and me, as I wanted to be certain I was putting myself in the best possible work situation.

By my first week at this new company, I had already blocked off time to hang out with my new "forced friend." But this wasn't the extent of peer-to-peer connectivity. Coworkers encouraged me to take breaks in the game room. At first, I would cautiously make my way over to the lounge, worried of how leaving my desk to socialize would come across to my supervisor. Later, I found out, breaks were highly encouraged in order to maintain productivity levels, as well as advocate for all employees from various departments to get to know each other. Everyone, from entry-level employees to the CEO of the company, was found engaging in a game of shuffleboard, ping-pong, or foosball at any given time of the day. Employees were bonding. We were learning from each other in a relaxed environment, taking advantage of peer-to-peer mentoring. The game room connected team members, boosted productivity, helped employees learn more about the business and job roles, and kept up company morale.

II. Flexibility: The Benefits of a Results-Only Work Environment

Workplace structures, including the dreaded eight-hour workday, need an update to retain Millennial talent. One change companies young and old are beginning to implement is workplace flexibility. The necessity of having an eight-hour workday is something businesses are reevaluating as they experiment with providing flexible working solutions. An option to work from home or remotely is one strategy employers are trying.

Having one-third of a 24-hour period devoted to work started during the era of the Industrial Revolution. In order to break up days spent laboring in factories, social reformer Robert Owen protested to compartmentalize days into tidy eight-hour factions: eight hours spent on work, eight hours for recreation, and eight hours to use for rest.[7]

In 1914, The Ford Motor Co. was one of the first to guarantee eight-hour workday shifts. When productivity rates improved for employees, other businesses instituted the new structure.[8]

The eight-hour day worked well because a lot of jobs needed employees to be present for physical labor, especially in factories. Employees also needed to be available in person to communicate faster, since cell phones and computers didn't exist. During that era, taking time to get in touch with someone could have slowed down productivity if a person wasn't available immediately. Today, however, a simple text message or email makes reaching out instantaneous. Though there are jobs in the 21st century that rely on employees being physically present, like construction jobs, retail workers, and roles within service industries, most contemporary positions do not require a linear eight-hour day. Here's how one modern-day company decided to change up this out-of-date structure.

At the start of the millennium, a multinational consumer electronics brand, known as Best Buy, was on the verge of trying something new to improve employee productivity. An idea to put into practice work autonomy sparked when Jody Thompson and Cali Ressler started to rework the human resources guidelines for the retailer. Curious to break up what the typical day had become and the lackluster work yielded during these hours, these two women created a new strategy: one where they were convinced positive results would ensue. The initiative would pay employees based on results instead of hours worked. The radical shift was dubbed ROWE (Results-Only Work Environment).[9]

Thompson and Ressler suggested implementing the radical structural shift in 2003, and the experiment was put into motion in 2005. Sociology professors at the University of Minnesota, Erin Kelly and Phyllis Moen, led the study. The guidelines were simple: employees could work from wherever made the most sense to them, change schedules without notifying a manger, and complete work at whatever hour of the day they chose. Workers would be held accountable solely for work they completed instead of time-based restrictions, like being 15 minutes late to work, taking too many sick days, or feeling pressured to keep working during vacation time off. As long as objectives were met, everything else was insignificant.

The extreme organizational shift yielded incredibly positive results for both employees and the business. Best Buy saw that the turnover of ROWE participants dropped by 45% percent, morale improved, and, for families, there was more balance between work and home life, reducing stress. Overall employee satisfaction improved as well. [10]

Nicholas Bloom, a professor at Stanford University, partnered with James Liang, co-founder of Ctrip, to conduct another study in 2014. Essentially a trial to see if Ctrip could save money by allowing employees to work from home, Bloom and Liang didn't expect one of the outcomes to be increased productivity. The experiment involved employees volunteering to work from home for nine months. Half of the employees who volunteered were assigned to telecommute, the other half made up the control group and remained in-office. At the conclusion of the nine-month test period, Bloom and Liang were pleasantly surprised by the data.

In a report by the *Harvard Business Review*, Bloom states, "The results we saw at Ctrip blew me away. Ctrip was thinking that it could save money on space and furniture if people worked from home, and that the savings would outweigh the productivity hit it would take when employees left the discipline of the office environment. Instead, we found that people working from home completed 13.5% more calls than the staff in the office did—meaning that Ctrip got almost an extra workday a week out of them. They also quit at half the rate of people in the office—way beyond what we anticipated. And, predictably, at-home workers reported much higher job satisfaction."[11] The financial perks for the business that came along with allowing employees more work flexibility included an estimated savings of $1,900 per employee during the nine-month period.

Inflexible schedules, such as demanding employees work within a strict window of time, enforcing regimented environments where eight hours minimum are mandatory, and making it so that project-driven assignments can only be accomplished from the office, have all caused dissatisfied and unhappy Millennial workers. These outdated workplace structures are one reason Generation-Y is not performing to the standards Boomers and Xers expect.

To make room for more flexibility, numerous Millennials are abandoning 9-5 roles, taking charge of their work by way of freelance, independent contractor, and consulting projects. In 2014, Millennials made up 38% of the freelance market, compared to 32% of those ages 35 and older, according to additional Upwork statistics. Interestingly, more and more employers are out-sourcing work to these freelancers, with 41% of hiring managers planning on increasing the use of freelancers by the years 2019-2020.

As the freelance economy grows, Millennials have the option to leave companies that are not maintaining pace with the life we want to achieve. Digital marketing writer, Julia Ingall, skillfully points out that, in relation to project-based work and the workforce today, you can "Mix and match your gigs, and voilà: You've got the ultimate balanced work lifestyle. In theory (assuming you have a laptop and reliable WiFi access), you could 'gig' from a mountainside perch, a log cabin, or your own living room (even in your pajamas)." Setting up a flexible role in lieu of a traditional office job, in some cases, works out better for Millennials. Where Generation-Y feels the need to leave their traditional job to take on the flexibility of freelance work, traditional jobs are now increasingly turning to freelancers for niche projects.

Four years into my professional career, I decided to transition back into writing, moving away from SEO. Landing a job at a well-known Beverly Hills retailer, I entered a company that relied on out-of-date structures, including a strict 10:00 a.m. to 6:00 p.m. workday. Feeling energetic and alert during my second week on the job, I decided to come into the office early, a decision later met with contention. Arriving at 8:30 and leaving at 4:30, the quiet office at the beginning of the day was the ideal space to focus and produce as much work as possible. Tapping into a zone of productivity was easy and seamless, as employees wouldn't start coming in until 10:00 a.m. I was able to accomplish tasks efficiently and turn out high-quality work that my supervisor was over the moon with. However, that supervisor was ultimately displeased that I couldn't produce the same quality of work within the regimented 10-6 timeframe, a timeframe that required working in an environment with heavy foot traffic, noise, and distractions. The option to work from home, though effective for work quality, was dismissed. How could I be expected to perform optimally in an atmosphere suited to squash creativity?

As time dragged on in this grayscale office, fluorescent lights bringing a harshness to worn carpet, I realized I was not the only dissatisfied employee. The general atmosphere was one of low morale. Mutters of employees leaving to find other work emphasized fast turnaround that managers eventually accepted. Though this particular office space had other issues, workplace flexibility could have helped on a couple of fronts. The company, which, at the time, was facing financial trouble, may have potentially saved money and resources by allowing more employees to work from home. Additionally, allowing a schedule where employees had the option to come into the office early or work later may have also helped boost productivity and overall job satisfaction, lowering attrition.

Evaluating how efficient a restrictive eight-hour day really is becomes necessary in keeping pace with the latest generation to occupy the labor force. Millennials have the reputation of being incapable of performing optimally. In reality, as a generation of overachievers, we are capable of surpassing our workplace goals, given the right circumstances.

Revisiting the results-only work environment experiment, if Millennials were assessed only on results, similar to how freelance assignments are evaluated, Boomers and Xers would have an easier time measuring the value of a Millennial employee. Having the option to set our own timeframes, within the boundaries of a greater deadline, and establish where we feel best working allows us to produce during our peak moments. This strengthens engagement with the project and enhances productivity, while saving businesses costs and frustration.

III. Feed Me Feedback When I Need It

Millennials want feedback, and we want it now. Timely and consistent critique of work, setting up short- and long-term goals, and meeting with Gen-Yers regularly has proven to be more valuable than mid-year and end-of-the-year assessments for this generation. Managers may credit Millennials as "attention sponges" and have concerns about providing a constant stream of feedback for each employee, but Millennials are persistent in wanting guidelines to help us succeed.

Receiving feedback when it is most relevant is imperative to motivate Millennials to work, not only with more confidence, but also to sustain our interests in and connectivity to a position. Bred as straight-A overachievers who have mastered maneuvering challenging coursework, jobs, and volunteer assignments simultaneously, we're always looking for the opportunity to transition our work ethics into the work world. In fact, that's what we've been preparing for our entire lives.

As we currently comprise the majority of the workforce, we need to know what we're working hard at and what the end outcome will be, as this was the structure outlined for us throughout high school and college. If we aren't set up to visualize our success in a job position—through innovative feedback strategies and workplace transparency—and have the right guidance to reach that success, our morale and work ethic will fall short.

Companies want Millennials to be innovative, yet business practices and procedures backslide at being modern and fresh, leaving very little room for Gen-Yers to introduce originality. While companies are fuzzy at providing timely and well-planned feedback out of bureaucratic habit, as well as the unwieldiness of how to restructure antiquated procedures, Millennials struggle to thrive in a traditional workplace setting. Knowing that Millennials *yearn* to improve in our respective industries, businesses without the know-how to provide a roadmap will leave Gen-Y employees disengaged.

Millennials are not shying away from critique, a characteristic that should be coveted. And once managers realize the value of this trait, they will be able to put into place effective strategies to activate our willingness and passion to grow with the company. By not engaging with Millennials however, assuming this generation will adapt to the behaviors of their Gen-X and Boomer predecessors, companies will continue to miss out on talent.

Imagine, for example, if Facebook tried to mimic the exact interface and functionality of MySpace when coming to life. Though both social media networks shared the common objective of being able to create online peer-to-peer connections, the two platforms achieved this very differently. While one may have been successful at first, the other fluctuated with the changing needs and demands of the people without altering the end goal. This is the same for Millennials. The aim of a workplace to drive success for the overall business hasn't changed, but the needs of the people have. And, in order for companies to easily meet their objectives, adaptation is crucial to get employees on board.

After spending a year with a digital marketing firm, assisting both with writing and SEO, I was excited to meet with supervisors for my mid-year evaluation. Two of my colleagues excitedly whispered that they had received pay increases and title changes, and I was certain, with my hard work and initiative, my assessment was going to go well. Throughout the year, I had volunteered to lead department-wide presentations on new marketing trends, earned four certifications in the industry, and partnered with the company to increase employee morale by helping with group events. I thought I had hit all of my goals, plus more.

Walking into a conference room, hair neatly placed in a bun, I sat facing the chief operations officer, the director, my supervisor, and the HR manager. Maintaining a confident stature and smile, I awaited feedback. Unfortunately, it wasn't what I was expecting. My participation was great, my knowledge and initiative were revered, and my ability to play well with others showed that I was a team player, concerned only for the good of the company. However, what they really wanted was for me to take on more client-facing roles, narrow the scope on what I was learning to more niche digital marketing trends, and spend more time working with new hires. I didn't hit their checkpoints and I wasn't eligible to receive a raise.

Flummoxed as to why these points weren't brought to my attention earlier...six to twelve months earlier, I asked, but they couldn't really provide me with a helpful response. They settled on the reasoning that my manager was overly busy and didn't have the time to check in as often as he would have liked. In essence, I was left to my own devices to figure out what the company needed from me, and, in this case, I had missed the mark.

Feeling depleted and let down, I aired my frustrations with co-workers and other people who, too, felt duped. For some employees who had stayed on board for two to three years, they expressed that this was normal, and that multiple people had articulated concerns in the past, pleading for some sort of reform. We all had worked so hard, from studying new marketing trends to putting in ample overtime, and the company didn't acknowledge our triumphs or steer us in the right direction if we were veering off from what they had wanted. Although we worked independently, without a team leader in place to provide solid feedback, our work missed the mark and we would stray off course. In this case, we were doing the work with all of the resources given to produce a great outcome, but it didn't matter, because managers never chimed in to voice if the work we were completing aligned with the company's needs.

By the time I left that particular position, the company had lost a member of their C-staff and multiple directors. Some departments were crumbling from overworked employees who were frustrated and always chasing what they could only guess the company wanted (and, oftentimes, they guessed incorrectly).

In the age of constant feedback, where businesses rely on consumer insights to improve the value of merchandise, services, and overall production, the same is needed for Millennial workers. Without routine check-ins to gauge morale, the quality of work being produced, and satisfaction on both employees' and business' end can suffer. As business leaders, let's not miss the mark on potential ways to better the company as a whole starting from the inside out.

Transparency: The Different Types & Why We Value It

Millennials have a penchant for workplace transparency. We seek it from organizational structure, which works in tandem with work culture and feedback, as well as the Internet and social media. Knowing whom we work for is significant when factoring in our company loyalty and engagement rate. Organizational structure and online news media are two very different forms of transparency, however.

How a company's hierarchy is set up internally or how a company breaks down chain-of-command communication barriers is something controlled from the inside. Yet, information Millennial workers come across on the web via social media, online news sources, or business review sites aren't entirely in the hands of companies. Gen-Y workers have access to information about a company's past, present, and even future, 24/7, and can use these insights to make informed decisions in relation to our values and goals.

When we look at organizational structure, this can refer to how a company orients communication between various levels of employees and the coordination, as well as distribution of tasks, according to employee tiers. In a traditional work landscape, sometimes lower-level employees are encouraged to take thoughts and ideas to their immediate supervisor; that supervisor can then connect with their supervisor if the thought or feedback is deemed worth sharing. Communication follows this pipeline or stops completely. An employee's suggestion may never reach its intended audience if one person vetoes the thought early on. In traditional office politics, there's little flexibility to break this unidirectional chain-of-communication, and this is what frustrates Millennials, who desire a more equalitarian way of sharing ideas.

Eliminating a wall of communication to encourage the thought leadership of Millennial employees makes an environment stimulating for this generation. We want our suggestions, feedback, and creativity to get a platform, and business goals to become more transparent during this process. Executing organizational transparency thus relies on C-level participation and their willingness to do away with more formal structural hierarchies.

Zappos is one radical example of this. In 2014, the plan to carry out flattening the workplace structure was put into effect by CEO Tony Hsieh. Referred to as holacracy, where there aren't any traditional managers, job titles, or formal bureaucratic structure, the intent is to get rid of corporate hierarchy all together by redistributing power across the organization.[12] Shifting to a holacracy is one extreme example of how a company can restructure an organization to make a more collaborative and transparent environment, but may be difficult for companies to execute immediately.

Additionally, the model is still being tested by Zappos, and success rates for this progressive restructuring are pending. Other things that can be implemented now, however, while making an incredible impact, include having an open design workspace, letting employees sit in on different departmental meetings, and keeping workers up to speed on the company's big financial successes or shortcomings, either through monthly or quarterly company-wide updates.

Coming from a department presentation, I walked the loop of the office, following the track and field style circuit of my workspace's design, to my desk. Uncertain of how to perform a task that was briefly discussed, I followed up with a co-worker, who was also unsure. We reached out to our manager next, who then directed us to go talk to the chief operating officer, as he was the expert on this subject. Approaching the C-level execs who sat on the floor with employees, everyone greeted me as I explained the situation. Eager to help, the COO pulled up a chair, urging me to sit and observe. He spent the next half hour going through the ins and outs of the task in a conversational approach. While seated next to him, I witnessed other employees whoosh by, some stopping to dunk a basketball in the mini hoop he had set-up on the edge of his desk, some to chat with the other executives.

Younger, newly established companies or older companies that adopt a start-up-style work environment favor the open concept workspace because this type of transparent setting fosters faster learning, teamwork, and trust, elements that a lot of businesses have trouble developing with Millennial employees. A spacious layout that's free of cubicles brings about an all-hands-on-deck atmosphere, while taking away the intimidation of approaching a manger or executive. At the particular company I worked for, collaboration flowed between employees and the C-level executives constantly.

This same company was also big on another tactic to keep employees in the loop: allowing workers to sit in on different meetings, regardless of whether or not it related to their specific job tasks. The objective was to show that, even though employees have varied responsibilities, everyone is operating to achieve the same business objective: financial success for the company. The more we know about one department's successes, or even failures, the better we can align our distinctive strengths to meet the goals of the company. And as HR-service provider Insperity reminds us of Millennials, "The motto will be: Succeed or fail, we're all in it together."

Another workplace reform start-up companies, or companies that adopt a start-up-like policy, enact is sharing company successes and shortcomings company wide. Businesses can acknowledge the achievements of departments or specific co-workers–depending on the size of the company–, review how the company measures up against competitors, welcome suggestions on how to improve company processes, and gauge overall company morale. Some businesses even introduce new hires, employees who have received promotions, and company philanthropic efforts. What's great about company-wide updates is that they keep everyone informed on how the brand is performing externally. Employees can be made aware of big changes, potential pitfalls, and a roadmap on how a business plans to succeed. In this way, we feel part of something bigger, and are more motivated to contribute to the overall success of the company.

When it comes to technology and transparency, the Internet, social media, and business review sites have made it so that businesses no longer have the advantage of keeping things private. The once-respected, on-a-need-to-know-basis-only attitude has shifted. Not only do we want to know how a business is performing compared to competitors, we also want to look at things like reputation, reliability of products and services, company treatment of employees and consumers, and how a brand is ethically and socially responsible.

User-generated company reviews and social media give Millennial job searchers these opportunities to learn as much about a company as possible and become informed. From creating an impression of a brand's reputation to understanding how a company uses social media to stay competitive, online channels play a considerable role in determining what type of brand a Millennial might want to do business with. In some cases, a Millennial job candidate may be visiting a business's social media channel for the first time. Not unlike meeting a new person, what a prospective Millennial employee reads and experiences online can immediately create a negative or positive first impression. This is why online reputations are important for brands that want to attract top Millennial talent.

In preparation for a preliminary phone interview, I started to conduct more research on a company that was interested in me. This was not only for the benefit of having facts available to show that I was a serious candidate, but also to make sure this was a company I wanted to pursue working with. After looking over the website and company values, my next step was to visit business review site, Glassdoor.

According to daily updated data from audience measurement tool Quantcast, by 2015, mid-September, Glassdoor drew in over 15 million monthly visitors from the U.S. alone, and those age 25-34—hitting part of the Millennial demographic—made up the largest group to visit the site. Xers came in at a close second, followed by Boomers. Why Glassdoor is so valuable is because current and former employees can anonymously voice concerns with management, work culture, company growth, etc. In turn, job candidates can assess how stable a company is, as well as get an idea of how employees are treated by looking at star ratings and reading personal experiences. Essentially, Glassdoor offers user reviews and recommendations for business-employee relations.

After reading a grab bag of negative comments for the job I would be interviewing for, including that management did not listen to employees, provide training opportunities, or show employee appreciation, I turned to social media to further explore. Using Twitter and LinkedIn, I gained insight into the company's financial stability, learned how conscientious and socially responsible they were, and, by looking at the brand's own social media pages, judged how adaptable and forward-thinking this company was compared to competitors—something to let me know if they had authority in their industry. In under an hour, I had generated my first impression. Similar to how I conducted research for my scheduled job interview, other Millennials use these resources to uncover need-to-know information about a business as well. With this type of transparency aided by the web, Gen-Y employees can now make a more informed decision before committing to a role.

Another way Millennials use company insights on the Web is by relying on the judgments and knowledge of our online communities. Innovative authors Jeanne C. Meister and Karie Willyerd, who provide profound and forward-thinking ideas in their book *The 2020 Workplace,* describe Millennials as "the most socially conscious generation since the 1960s."[13] Generation-Y makes sure to take into account a brand's social responsibility before signing up to work with them and, in this way, a company's reputation has a huge influence on current workers and prospective candidates. If a business is trending in the news for the wrong reasons, and we see an ample amount of peers protesting online, this can reshape our views. Not only will these brands lose our consumer loyalty, they will also lose our trust and engagement as employees.

When logging on to any of my social media channels, from Instagram, Facebook, Twitter, or even Snapchat, my feeds always contain the latest national and international news, as well as community responses to the most viral stories. Quite frequently an update targets irresponsible marketing from a brand or a company's social irresponsibility. From corporations like agriculture biotechnology giant Monsanto,[14] to fashion retailer, American Apparel,[15] Millennials are in the loop, regardless of industry, service, or product. And the way we respond to these brands starts by sharing as much information with our peers as quickly as possible. This mode of transparency forces companies into the public eye quickly, and is used as an effort to educate and pursue change.

Millennials are forcing this shift to openness in the workforce because we not only want to be held accountable for our own work, but we also want businesses to be held accountable for theirs. And, unsurprisingly, the pursuit of transparency via organizational structure and online communication works. For better or worse, the reputation of a company will stream into public consciousness, and the better the public image of a company, the more qualified and engaged workers will be attracted to working for that brand. Thus, company branding is key for workplaces that are in constant competition to attract Millennial experts.

After compiling my research to use as the subject of my follow-up questions for my phone interview, I set up a time to speak with a representative from the company who was interested in me. The 15-minute call, though brief, gave me further insight into the business, and reinforced online findings. The company's goals were vague, the HR management hinted there were communication gaps across departments, and the job role itself didn't rely on teamwork to meet the needs of the business, but instead created an every-person-for-himself/herself mentality. I was able to make the decision not to move forward with this brand, even though they were interested in my particular skill sets, because of my research.

Defining Digital Natives: How Technology Changes the Work Landscape

Millennials are "digital natives." We work naturally with technology, since we are the first generation to grow up with it. We are able to use our inherent know-how to operate any device, ranging from desktop, laptop, tablet, or mobile phone; stay up-to-date with a bevy of trends, including business, marketing, social media, and entertainment news; as well as come up with fresh ideas on how technology can connect us like the creators of peer-to-peer services Lyft and Uber, or AirBnB.

"Digital immigrants,"[16] like Boomers and Xers, are starting to adapt to the rapid-fire technology upgrades by learning the ins and outs of tools already quotidian to Gen-Yers. Setting up a Facebook page or learning what a hashtag is and how it connects the flow of online conversations are examples that benchmark where prior generations are when it comes to web communications. Millennials, on the other hand, are already past these evolutions.

Having a proclivity for technology and social media trends increases the value of having a Millennial on a workforce team, especially in an era where big businesses are starting to digitize internal processes, as well as use advanced technologies to remain competitive. However, the gap in skill sets can sometimes decelerate the rate at which new technology is absorbed on the job. This can disengage a Millennial employee whose expectations rely on having modern tools to perform, while leaving Boomers and Xers exasperated.

Speaking with a Generation-X human resources manager who specializes in adult learning and training she admitted to me that her company was not progressive when it came to updating their technology and resources. For example, digitizing documents for new hire orientation was problematic, as many of her department leads were uncertain of the benefit, while her Millennial employees grew excited at the idea of having less paperwork to maintain, not only for convenience but for social consciousness.[17]

Her plan involved having an online 3-D flipbook, where information such as job functions, benefits, procedures, and company contacts could be uploaded through a drag and drop system. The plan would ultimately save on resources and costs. Boomers and Generation-X members who were unable to grasp the significance of modernizing new hire procedures dismissed the suggestion. The understanding wasn't there between the older generation and those newer to the workforce. This disconnect can be detrimental, not only to businesses who aren't flexible in making processes easier by way of technology, but to Millennial employees who work best in stimulating digital environments that are modern and, whenever possible, eco-friendly.

What prior generations are struggling to tap into are the coming-of-age technological advancements. Instead they remain stuck in learning the functionalities of older software and apps. Operating Microsoft Office Suite products remains a challenge for some Boomers and Gen-Xers, and is only one example of how older generations are falling behind.

What's important to realize is that, as businesses want to use digital experiences to establish a new consumer reality, the backend of the business also needs to be technologically up-to-date. For internal processes, there's ample room for improvement, whether that's taking on a project management system, understanding how the Cloud operates, or even digitizing day-to-day tasks like signing documents with help from a service like EchoSign. These modern developments help to save on costs and establish a more eco-friendly work environment, the latter catering to Millennials' social consciousness.

Staying up-to-date is no secret to staying ahead. The four technologies forward-thinking businesses are executing for better consumer and employee experiences include social media, mobile, analytics, and Cloud advancements (SMAC).[18] As these digital upgrades are at the helm of progressive businesses, they also work to attract and retain Millennial talent.

In my mid-20s, I took a break from the corporate world. Even the businesses that featured endless perks and a casual environment did not live up to what I was looking for in a productive work environment. Taking on freelance projects that catered to my creativity and allowed for total control over my work schedule gelled with my Millennial wants and desires. I could work at any hour of the day and from wherever: my living room floor, a bar and grill, the library, or a park. I didn't have to spend months attempting to meet goals to satisfy vague assessments. My clients' feedback, paychecks, and referrals were the only things I relied on for success.

Early on in my freelance career, I noticed something interesting. Working for predominantly Generation-X and Baby Boomer entrepreneurs, these business owners were unable to establish workflow and cash flow because they didn't have the technical skills needed to run their business. LinkedIn was an unheard of, uncharted territory, that would take hours to explain, describing how a hashtag works to populate search queries on social media was a task that necessitated creating a guide, and teaching business owners how to use presentation tools like PowerPoint to produce a sales pitch was a novel strategy. I had found a market where older generations who used to be top of their field had lost footing, due to the evolving technological landscape.

As the digital era continues to drive so many new innovations Millennials can easily be trained on digital updates. The challenge is getting businesses to invest in

Millennial talent by implementing flexibility, training, and a stimulating work culture. Once a company does this, Millennials can work hand-in-hand with older generations to teach technological nuances. This builds leadership, teamwork, and trust, skills that set the foundation for a business to succeed.

Dispelling the Myth

When it comes to Millennials and our on-the-job characterization, we have been labeled as disloyal to companies, disengaged from tasks, and difficult to work with. We want endless perks, only to leave a company after a couple of years or fewer. In reality, though our workplace needs differ from former generations, we are willing to work hard, given the proper support, to develop our strengths.

What Millennials need in the workplace include meaningful projects, team bonding, modernity in the form of flexibility and feedback, and transparency. As Meister and Willyerd sum up nicely, "Millennials view work as a key part of life, not a separate activity that needs to be 'balanced' by it."[19] With that thought in mind, Millennials are willing to overachieve, given the ideal blend of structure, mentorship, and team support to pioneer a forward-thinking mindset.

Additional Ways Companies Can Attract Millennial Talent

1. **Encourage workplace diversity:** According to an insightful 2014 Glassdoor study, "67% of active and passive job-seekers say that when they're evaluating companies and job offers, it is important to them that the company has a diverse workforce."[20]

   As the most culturally diverse generation, Millennials are dedicated to having more diversity in all facets of our lives, including the workplace. Work cultures that are diverse tend to be attractive to quality employees. When a company hires people from all backgrounds, this signals to Generation-Y that they are progressive and on-board with eschewing former biases that once homogenized business culture.

2. **Be Flexible with Vacation Time:** More and more companies are implementing unlimited vacation time off. This can help Millennials set their own pace and schedule to produce quality work. There is one disadvantage to this perk, and it is not the one you're thinking. Companies find that with unlimited vacation policies, employees are underutilizing their time off, unsure of how much time is appropriate to take.

Laura Vanderkam, one of the top authors on time management and productivity, expertly describes solutions for this, one of which includes having managers "lead by example," and take vacations themselves. Vanderkam also mentions incentivizing the act, applauding those who are able to commit to checking out and recharging.[21]

These strategies work best for optimizing performance, as well as providing a flexible work environment where Millennials work autonomously without burning out.

3. **Invest In Additional Learning Opportunities:** Millennials are the poorest generation in 25 years. Using this knowledge, you can help Generation-Y take advantage of paid learning opportunities on your dime. Companies that capitalize on tuition reimbursement plans show that they are willing to invest in their employees' career growth.[22]

David Melancon, CEO of btr, a platform that ranks companies based on holistic performance, even brilliantly suggests to jobseekers to, when interviewing, inquire about education and development.

He reminds Millennials, "You've put a lot of effort and investment into your education and it's possible—

especially if this is an entry-level job—that you may not yet be making a salary commensurate with that."

"Some companies realize that and offer assistance in paying off student loans, or assist in furthering your education. Do they have programs that allow you to continue your education? Understanding the company's point of view on education—past and future—as well as how it implements that POV in benefits is important."[23]

8

The F-Word

Truth Bomb:

According to the Center for American Progress, women accounted for just 16% of all the directors, executive producers, producers, writers, cinematographers, and editors who worked on the top-grossing 250 domestic films of 2013, and were just 28% of all off-screen talent in broadcast television programs during the 2012-13 prime time season. When, however, there are more women behind the camera or at the editor's desk, the representation of women on-screen is better. Films written or directed by women consistently feature a higher percentage of female characters with speaking roles. As it stands, however, women's image on-screen is still overwhelmingly created by men.[1]

Boys will be Boys: Rape Culture & Victim Blaming

As someone who was sexually assaulted, I understand what it is like to have others view me as a victim. I was a college sophomore who naively escorted an intoxicated male partygoer to the restroom. He lured me in to make out, which started off consensual, but then he wanted to go much further, much quicker, pushing me against the sink and either pinning my arms down or manipulating my hands to touch his genitalia. I was fortunate enough to pull away from his grasp, and reported the incident to the campus police at the university I was attending. They were quick to take action and had a zero-tolerance policy for sexual abuse and misconduct, expelling my attacker.

A friend of mine, however, pleaded with me to do something more. She wanted me to go a step further, and file a police report. She had been raped a year earlier on campus. Passed out in her dorm room after a party, a male friend snuck in and raped her. She woke up to him inside of her, assuring her that everything would be OK. Her attacker had had a longstanding crush, and broke into her room to act out his fantasy.

She was a well-loved, doe-eyed blonde, but never felt comfortable reporting the incident because she knew it would create a confrontational setting among her and her friends, since the guy who had raped her was also just as admired on campus. Plus, she excused his behavior since he was intoxicated. All of this seemed to swell to a rage when

121

she vehemently pressed me to file charges against the person who'd assaulted me. She wanted her redemption, and she didn't want me to live in the same regretful state that she currently found herself in.

The truth is that my situation could have been a lot more frightening and the outcome much worse. Though I did not want to press charges, school counselors encouraged me to talk about it, friends were passionate about me taking action, and the university became much more stealthy at educating students on how to avoid situations or report them if, inevitably, they had occurred. My school, colleagues, friends, and professors were all supportive and helpful, a privilege that I now realize is not always available to other teens and twenty-somethings attending a private or public institution.

I think about this after reading the conflict-ridden *Rolling Stone* article that had intensely hit the online space in 2015. The title of the article at once triggered a knee-jerk reaction of uneasiness, anger, and the need to immediately do something. "A Rape On Campus: A Brutal Assault and Struggle for Justice at UVA," by Sabrina Erderly, was the story of "Jackie's" alleged gang rape. The grisly re-telling of then-freshman Jackie's assault by members of a campus fraternity reopened debates on how responsibly student assaults are handled on college campuses nationwide.[2]

Though *Rolling Stone* later retracted the story, as many purported facts were untrue, this does not diminish the fact that rape and sexual assault cases in school settings are often handled poorly. In this instance, the details of Jackie's alleged story contained many holes, ranging from the timeline of when the attack happened to the workplace of her alleged attacker. Was this a case of PTSD? Did Jackie repress memories? Though her story may never fully be explained, what is frightening is how many students stepped forward to admit that they had been raped, assaulted, and battered on the University of Virginia campus. Now that Jackie's story is discredited, believing other rape survivors can be more difficult, making their investigations subject to more scrutiny, hesitation to act, and victim blaming.

A large part of why women are uncomfortable sharing their stories has to do with the fear of not being believed, experiencing rejection from peers, and feeling personally responsible for the attack. I even debated whether to let my assailant go, afraid that I would be blamed for openly trusting a stranger. I did not want his actions to be a reflection of my intelligence, especially in a world where women and their intellect are so frequently questioned. I eventually conceded, however, and, though I may have had a happy ending when it came to the support of my peers, parents, and teachers, there are plenty of women who remain silent, out of fear of being isolated in their communities.

One underlying issue is that rape is consistently perceived as a victim-based problem, a punishment for women not conforming to male-centric social ideas. Not wearing appropriate attire, flirting, drinking too much, or engaging in "promiscuous behavior" are examples of reasons that have been used against girls and women to undermine an attack. Trivializing comments, including "What was she wearing?" or "Boys will be boys" place the onus of attack on women, instead of owning that men, and men alone, are responsible for the act.

Gen-Yers are bringing attention to this flawed thinking. Artist and activist, Emma Sulkowicz, for example, protested the aftermath of her alleged rape in an internationally-reaching demonstration by carrying her dorm room mattress with her at all times on campus. A student at Columbia University, Sulkowicz, dubbed "mattress girl," wanted to stand up against rape by creating action out of her university's inaction. Three years after, she also published a graphic video online, "Ceci N'est Pas Un Viol," which translates to "This is Not a Rape," which features her and a hired male actor displaying just how easily rape can occur. [3]

Understanding how common it can be for a woman to receive pushback when verbalizing that she has been raped or assaulted has led Gen-Yers to advocate for social reform. With the UVA incident, the details were foggy, but online communities started the #IStandWithJackie protest.

Even if Jackie's retelling of events was untrue, and her alleged rape never happened, other UVA students stepped forward to share their own rape stories.

Examining data from the Bureau of Justice Statistics, only 20% of female student survivors age 18-24 report to law enforcement[4] that they have been raped or assaulted. We can surmise that this number is so low because women are afraid to speak up. With very little, if any, repercussions for a victim's rapist(s) coupled with immense backlash for the survivor, fear ensues and what's known as rape culture persists. So, what is rape culture?

A phrase brought to life at the pinnacle of the Millennial women's rights movement, rape culture is defined as a society that accepts sexual abuse, misconduct, and mistreatment of women as the norm based on societal views of gender roles. The common colloquial phrase "boys will be boys," noted earlier, is an example where males are allowed the privilege to evade discipline for actions that are harmful either to themselves, society, or women. As with the case of Emma Sulkowicz, her assailant never received punishment. In other cases of assault on campus, men who attack women commonly receive a light sentence, which sometimes simply equates to suspension from school for a year. The victim, on the other hand, as we often see in these stories, is isolated from peers, receives little guidance or compassion from administrators, and faces subsequent bullying and persecution. This can lead to emotional instability and, in some cases, suicide.

Sulkowicz's story was only one example of gross sexual misconduct that wasn't handled appropriately. Others have surfaced, indicating how endemic rape and sexual assault is, and oftentimes the response is that victims should assume responsibility for their actions, not the male perpetrator. The Steubenville case in Ohio is another instance of this.

One August evening, a then-16-year-old girl went to a high school party. The following morning, she woke up in a basement, naked, with a blanket thrown over her. Three guys were there. The party had escalated to a terrifying scene, and social media later revealed how and what had happened. After later testifying, the victim recounted that after consuming a mixed drink and Smirnoff she felt unusually drunk. Leaving the first party with a group of other students, including one male friend she trusted, they had headed to party number two. At some point she blacked out, only briefly recalling vomiting.

Social media and text messages revealed that her clothes had been stripped and two high school students had penetrated her with their fingers. They transported her naked, immobile body, photographing themselves in the process. When she came to the next morning, her phone and underwear were missing, and she wasn't aware of what had occurred, until social media posts were shared with her later.[5]

The Steubenville case in Ohio was picked up by media. Photos of her being abused circulated via texts, Facebook posts, Tweets, and email. The event received a bevy of mixed reactions, including her town shaming her for her conduct.

Placing the blame on the victim, otherwise known as victim-shaming or victim-blaming, is a common experience for women who are attacked by men. This takes the responsibility off of the perpetrator and attributes it to the injured party. Now efforts are being put into place to draw attention to and put a stop to this. At the conclusion of the Steubenville case, one of the perpetrators who was found guilty was able to return to high school and rejoin his football team.

Though we are still working on instituting fair measures to protect women universally, there have been some successes. Several college campuses, for example, are swapping out "No Means No" campaign language for "Yes Means Yes." The new jargon can be found on posters with other declarative statements that highlight what consent is, such as "No is Not Yes," and "Drunk is Not Yes."

California Governor Jerry Brown even signed legislation that reforms sexual education programs in the state. With this, the burden of proof is no longer the responsibility of the victim or the accusing party, but shifts to the accused. The idea is that not objecting will no longer be grounds for consent, which can be tricky if, say, a party were to rape someone who was passed out. The passed-out victim in that case would not be able to object. Would that count as consent? Under this legislation, absolutely not, and those terms are clear from the beginning. Only if both parties "enthusiastically" agree, and give permission by verbally communicating yes, is the activity considered consensual.

With these modifications, the goal is to make sex safe for all parties involved, including women who are most likely to be caught in the dismissive retorts of "boys will be boys," and "she was asking for it." Laura Dunn, executive director of not-for-profit national organization SurvJustice stated, "Traditionally we've focused on a lack of consent as someone fighting off an attacker. You looked for evidence of resistance. We only talked about what consent was not, which is not a very helpful paradigm. From the victims' side, it says we have to resist. But even looking at this from the perspective of someone being accused, the traditional definition is telling them that it's O.K. to do this until the victim says 'no'. That's not really a helpful definition for them either, because it can really be too late at that point. With affirmative consent, it's simple. Consent is consent."[6] Now, as California has adopted this legislation, other states are following suit, reprogramming behavior to actually understand what consensual sex is in an effort to promote consent and safety, and, by proxy, eliminate the victim-blaming mentality.

Breaking Socializations with the World Wide Web

Millennials are savvy at drawing attention to social justice issues by staging online protests, blogging, and producing videos. By using social media to propel feminism, or equal rights for women, and suppress gender stereotyping of men, people are introduced to empowered messaging every day, prompting easier exploration of these topics on the Web.

Compared to Gen-Xers and Baby Boomers who didn't have the Internet or social media growing up, the ease of information exchange allows for faster dissemination of news. Not surprisingly, social media channels are referenced as primary news outlets for Millennials. In fact, according to The American Press Institute, 88% of Millennials get their news from Facebook, and 57% of those who use Facebook as a news source do so at least once a day. Reddit, Twitter, and YouTube are other online options to disperse information; and the younger the Millennial, the more likely they are to use multiple social channels for news insights.[7]

This information exchange infused with the daily habits of Millennials prompts Millennial writers and activists to use their digital lives as a way to initiate discussions. Gen-Y video blogger, Laci Green, is one example of someone who uses engaging videos to educate audiences on the biases of masculine-feminine gender roles, while explaining how and why these roles exist. Her video "Why I'm a...FEMINIST *gasp*" received over three million YouTube views alone, while also generating plays on Upworthy and *Huffington Post*. She reminds us in a seemingly infinite list why she's a feminist and why we should be as well.

Pointing out objectifying, as well as sexist facets of our culture, Green calls to mind unfair treatment that society should be examining regularly. Examples include how boobs are used to sell everything, yet breastfeeding is prohibited in a lot of public spaces; men occupy top-rung positions not only in politics, but in nearly every position across the world; women are encouraged to place unrealistic expectations on their appearance. Because of her empowering video, Green has become one of the most well known Millennial vloggers and public speakers, who's as candid as she is relatable.

Marinashutup is another vlogger who tackles conversations on feminism through her series *Feminist Fridays*. Her video "Feminism 101: A Crash Course" is one example of an expert educational resource. She discusses key vocabulary terms like patriarchy, meaning a social system in place that values masculinity over femininity;

intersectionality, which is when our identities as well as systems of oppression overlap (the term was coined by Kimberlé Crenshaw and is used by Black feminists); Trans Inclusivity, defined as including trans women in the discussion for equal rights and safe spaces. Marinashutup includes ample others, encouraging followers to stay up to date and informed.

Despite the surge in these progressive posts from Generation-Yers like Green, Marinashutup and plenty of others, trolls or online users who seek to start conflict by posting inflammatory remarks also frequently target social media channels and comment feeds. Internet trolls can be especially predatory and aggressive. Here's one example of how I had to confront an Internet troll when sticking up for a friend ...

After returning home from a trip to Vegas, I reviewed my "album" of photos I had taken on my phone. Selecting the best ones of my girlfriends and me, I applied the appropriate filters and shared on Facebook, as well as other social channels. A photo that drew the most attention featured a group of us posed in party dresses on the Vegas strip. Almost immediately, a married male Facebook friend shared a distasteful remark about one of the women's breasts and what he wanted to do with them, crossing into the territory of sexual harassment.

She immediately flagged the comment and asked me to talk with him since he was my online connection.

Promptly deleting his objectifying remark, I sent him a private message explaining how he had made a woman feel uncomfortable. His retort telling both her and me to put on our "big-girl panties" and suck it up was, in part, unexpected, yet unsurprising.

Millennials are working to address this toxic male attitude head on. In my case, several friends who had spotted his initial comment before I removed it expressed disapproval and jumped to iterate how the remarks were objectifying and inappropriate by actually replying to him. When he didn't take personal ownership, I removed him as a friend. In some examples Millennials have even gone as far as reporting misconduct to a perpetrator's employer or by sharing the misconduct across additional platforms in an attempt to bring more attention to it to iterate what's right and what's wrong. In my case, cutting off contact with the person was enough.

In order to disrupt this type of gender-biased behavior, Millennials draw attention to it publically and group together to address the issue. With social platforms anyone can document acts of sexism. *10 Hours of Walking NYC as a Woman,* depicting street harassment is a well-known example of this.

This short video looked at catcalling, the act of men approaching women with unsolicited greetings, by following a woman making her way through the streets of New York. Remarks like "Smile," "Hey, Beautiful," or a wolf whistle bolted at her everywhere she turned.[8] On the surface these remarks or actions might seem harmless, even complimentary, however, men know that catcalling typically won't result in a romantic pairing. In this way catcalling becomes more of a way for a man to humiliate and assert power over a woman publically, knowing that she can oftentimes do very little about it.

One of the most supportive follow-ups to *10 Hours of Walking NYC as a Woman* was the #DudesGreeting-Dudes online movement. The campaign showed the silliness of confusing cat-calling with flattery. Elon James White who started the online initiative, talked to BuzzFeed News, exclaiming, "After the now infamous video came out last week there was a flood of critiques around the idea that dudes were just greeting women and I found them to be disingenuous at best."[9]

White's idea argues that if these are greetings lacking in predatory intent, men should say them to each other. With this, he gave humorous examples of how men can approach other men sharing on Twitter the same lines men use to greet women. He kicked off the campaign by first tweeting "These women don't get it. Y'all just want to say hi. What's wrong with hi?!?! So let's just leave them out completely #DudesGreetingDudes." Other tweets followed, saying, "You see a dude looking all hard & shit. Roll up on him like 'Aye yo, smile, son. Damn.' BRING SUNSHINE

TO HIS DAY. #dudesgreetingdudes." The movement picked up online, explaining the real objective of catcalling.

Big brands are also using videos to publically draw attention to gender bias. The #LikeAGirl campaign by Always took a different approach to get the message across compared to *10 Hours of Walking NYC as a Woman*, brilliantly tackling socialized perceptions of girls as weaker. The short shows how worldviews about girls and women are negatively internalized, and works to reverse this poor thinking by reclaiming the phrase "like a girl."[10] The campaign notes that at puberty girls' confidence plummets. By the time we're older, men and women alike agree that the phrasing "like a girl" is an insult. And when the video asks multiple people to do something like a girl, for example "run like a girl" or "hit like a girl," men and women complete the action weakly and poorly.

Young girls are asked to complete the same tasks and they surprisingly run naturally, or throw a ball as if they were on an open field. They haven't been affected by the stereotyping yet. When one of the campaign producers highlights the negative implications of the colloquialism, teens and women who are older are asked if they want to redo their attempts at what it means to complete an action like a girl, showcasing how they would really act if they were running or throwing a ball instead of what they're expected to do. The video ends with the statement, "Why can't 'run like a girl' also mean win the race?"

When Millennials rally to confront these issues through video, social media, and blogs, responses are shared across the Web through the same channels. Sometimes the responses aren't in favor of the movement however, even when the messaging is innovative and inspiring.

Women Against Feminism is a social media campaign that travelled across platforms Twitter, Tumblr, Facebook, and others. Women participate in a selfie-style protest openly communicating their angst over modern-day feminism.[11] The movement was met with criticism, especially as these women are unaware of the freedoms they currently have due to feminism, including the right to safely protest. Additionally, on a more comical note, Women Against Feminism inspired a parody protest called "Confused Cats Against Feminism," toying with the belief that the group simply doesn't grasp the ideology of modern-day feminism, thanks, in part, to many mainstream misconceptions.

I remember in the early 2000s, proudly declaring myself a feminist before the word grew to its heightened, reclaimed meaning. I had repeatedly received backlash from both male and female friends who didn't quite understand. I was just learning about the word myself, only knowing one thing: I wanted to be treated as an equal. I was ridiculed, since I didn't fit the image of a feminist at that time—I was a 4-inch-heel-clad, lover of all things high-fashion, bubbly college student. I didn't meet the criteria to be taken seriously as a feminist, and it wasn't until 2012-2013 that the term became increasingly more popular and the masses more informed.

Before reigniting this, feminism was misconceived in popular culture as a man-hating movement that attracted women who refused to shave or accept chivalry as an adequate standard of treatment. Now Millennials have a more inclusive view of feminism that not only includes women's rights, but the elimination of gender stereotyping that affects men. People are in turn coming together to eliminate the former image of feminism in hopes to clear up those misconceptions and recognize that these rights apply to all women and men globally.

Destigmatizing the Fear of Women's Rights Globally

Feminism continues to take precedence in Gen-Y conversations as we examine cultural injustices worldwide. We're making people aware about the need for education for women globally, rape and the unwanted pregnancies that follow, and how men, especially those in political power, use their privilege to dictate decisions that affect women's bodies. We're also avidly discussing the suppression of women by men based on religious rhetoric. Globally, women remain, on many levels, powerless.

Millennials who are part of Western Culture have it easier in expressing the need for change. Gen-Yers of other cultures, especially in developing nations, experience harsher by-products of gender biases that can lead to extreme violence, and unfortunately this violence is endemic. From sexual abuse of young girls and women to acts like acid attacks that handicap those who are assaulted for life, these things often occur when a woman defies a male whom by societal standards, is considered the supreme authority figure.

Acknowledging the varying degrees of privilege that women in Western culture have, compared to minority women or women living in other parts of the world are important. In this way we can inform others that men and women do not live in an egalitarian society and on a global scale feminism and womanism isn't about hairy armpits or bashing men. It's about confronting things that do not necessitate progress on the overarching spectrum of gender equality. Take the experience of Malala for example and her harrowing fight for education for girls.

Dressed in a navy and white school uniform, Malala boarded her school bus in Swat Valley. Singing resonated from students who were being transported to their classroom. The afternoon would be full of learning, a practice not acceptable for girls. In moments to come that very act of wanting to learn would put Malala's life in jeopardy.

Since the age of 11, Malala had already established herself as an outspoken advocate for girls' education, even in face of Taliban violence. Her diary entries conveyed someone fearless in moving forward for the sake of progress. When two men pulled over Malala's bus on October 9, 2012, and asked for her specifically, her life's mission would be cemented in history books.

At that moment, as she was discovered on the bus by the Taliban, she squeezed the hand of a classmate. She was shot three times at point-blank range, including a gunshot to the head, which travelled from her cheek to her shoulder. Miraculously she survived and, now, with international support, continues her fight for equality hungrier than before.

Malala Yousafzai illustrates how fundamentally necessary it is for girls to receive an education in order to be able to support themselves independently in her country. "Our men think earning money and ordering around others is where power lies. They don't think power is in the hands of the woman who takes care of everyone all day long, and gives birth to their children," Malala notes in her book, *I Am Malala: The Girl Who Stood Up for Education and Was Shot by the Taliban*.[15] Being the youngest Nobel Peace Prize recipient, Malala is the Millennial face for girls' rights activism and speaks globally about the support and resources still needed to help liberate women in countries where earning an education in a safe environment should not at any cost be a privilege exclusive to boys and men.

Despite powerful Gen-Yers like Malala, developing countries continue to struggle to end gender disparity and close the education gap between males and females. According to data from the 2012 World Development Report on Gender Equality and Development from The World Bank, 31 million girls were out of school, and wage gaps averaged 20%.[16] Without education, girls are forced to rely on men for survival before they even reach adulthood. In developing countries, this could mean being locked into underage marriage where girls are sexually abused, exploited, and physically and mentally assaulted. By allowing girls the same access to education as boys, however, we can reduce violence and improve economic growth, and with those luxuries comes an empowered race, which men fear most.

On April 14, 2014, Christian and Muslim schoolgirls rested in their hostels in Borno State, Nigeria. What began as a restful evening, ended in warfare and turmoil. Gunfire broke out, disrupting the night, and the hostels were set ablaze. Outside, buses and vans loaded with Islamic extremists under the terrorist group Boko Haram, waited as girls age 15 to 18 emptied out of their dormitory in panic. The girls were then herded into the vehicles, kidnapped, and taken into captivity. Boko Haram translates to mean "Western or Non-Islamic education is a sin."

That night, and into the morning of April 15, 2014, 276 girls were kidnapped. While 57 managed to escape a little over a year later, 219 girls are still unaccounted for. The campaign #BringBackOurGirls launched across social media uniting efforts with even First Lady Michelle Obama utilizing online protests to incite action.

The abasement of girls' and women's rights is not only a Western/American problem, but a worldwide phenomenon. Violence against women can be curbed, education opportunities can be created, and the regulations put in place that legislate the treatment of girls and women as second-class citizens can be banned. Thanks to social media, Gen-Y has been able to plug in and record gender disparity internationally. Documenting realities that would otherwise go unseen and using our ability to share information freely is one way we can involve others in what's happening worldwide. With help from peer-to-peer connections online, we are forming not only a web of communication, but a web of action.

Feminism Draws in Celebrity Involvement

Women's rights movements have a long and influential history. Scores of women have fought for necessities such as the right to vote, fair working conditions, improved wages, and the right to an education, all of the above being privileges primarily rewarded to Western women. While Rosie the Riveter is a culturally well-recognized emblem that's been associated with feminism, a few real-life historical suffragettes include Ida B. Wells, Susan B. Anthony, Lucy Stone, and Sojourner Truth, among many others.

Progress has been made and, as the feminism camp continues to evolve, contemporary celebrities are proving there is still more advancement that needs to occur in this ever-changing and dynamic landscape of equality.

Quite a few entertainers, both men and women, have used their platform to share pivotal views. Famous female celebrities include Emma Watson, Beyoncé, and Mindy Kaling, while male A-listers are Aziz Ansari, Joseph Gordon Levitt, and Louis C.K. Those are only a nominal number of well-known public figures, with a variety of listicles routinely populating the web space introducing newly discovered celebrity feminists. Emma Watson has been especially prolific in educating and mobilizing fans, encouraging both genders to fight for equality between the sexes.

As a prominent cultural figure who has a multi-generational fan base, Watson delivered a game-changing speech on feminism for the United Nations. Given the moniker of U.N. Women Goodwill Ambassador, she delivered a brilliant 11-minute-long speech covering global women's issues, as well as how the "masculine" archetype, also inherent in gender bias, affects society as a whole. She explored how women are conditioned to maintain one ideal, while men are strongly encouraged to live up to another, thus creating imminent gender disparity. As a result, it is common that each gender feels the pressure to conform to the roles of the archetype that they are assigned, which can lead to mental health issues and, in some cases, violence, as men will feel the need to assert their strength, masculinity, and dominance over women, especially in developing countries. In her impassioned dialogue, Watson discussed how she has witnessed some of her male friends become susceptible to this gender stereotyping, serving as a trigger to mental unhealthiness, in some cases including depression.

Watson's speech was delivered to introduce the HeForShe campaign, with one of the intentions being to mobilize millions of boys and men to advocate on behalf of ending gender inequalities between themselves and female peers. In addition to Watson painting feminism as an all-inclusive movement, where men have also been negatively affected by systemic gender stereotyping and gender roles, Watson also enlightened peers as to the definition of feminism, stating, "For the record, feminism by definition is the belief that men and women should have equal rights and opportunities. It is the theory of the political, economic and social equality of the sexes." She discouraged audiences against taking part in the tossed-around misconception that feminism is a man-hating movement, avoiding the "us versus them" idea and proving that feminism is a mutually relevant stance. Her mission was successful; countless male celebrities used the HeForShe hashtag on social media, including Harry Styles, Russell Crowe, Emile Hirsch, and Chris Colfer, along with others, using accompanying signs and posters to showcase their solidarity.[17]

Iconic singer Beyoncé has embraced feminism publicly, as well. Rousing women across all generations to participate in the all-inclusive movement by defining feminism and educating audiences on women's rights, Beyoncé is one entertainer who has mitigated the fear and misconception people previously had about the movement.

The surprise launch of her self-titled platinum album features a sexually liberated, powerful woman, speaking to generations of women suppressed by a patriarchal system. Beyoncé's *On The Run* tour with husband Jay-Z included a backdrop of neon-lit lettering stalwartly spelling out 'Feminist.' "We have to teach our boys the rules of equality and respect, so that, as they grow up, gender equality becomes a natural way of life. And we have to teach our girls that they can reach as high as humanly possible," Beyoncé remarked.

Celebrities of this generation are now increasingly self-aware not only of how they affect millions of viewers, but also how the industry plays a role in manipulation and sexism. Knowing this, both male and female A-listers confront misogynistic tendencies prevalent in Hollywood.

On red carpets, for example, numerous women celebrities are insistent on being asked the same questions as men, questions that evoke thoughtful responses that underline their talents, individuality, and character strengths. This movement, referenced as #AskHerMore on social media, abruptly puts a stop to inquiring solely about the designer dress a woman is wearing. This takes the focus off of exclusively highlighting beauty and beauty practices. Even 360-degree rotating stages to a get full view of a woman's gown or using a mini camera to draw attention to the color of nail polish women sport are generating backlash.

Cate Blanchett drew attention to the E! News Glam Cam at the 2014 Screen Actors' Guild Awards, which attempted to follow the length of her Givenchy gown from bottom to top. She immediately questioned the objectifying tactic, famously asking, "Do you do that to the guys?" On the same red carpet, actress Elisabeth Moss shared her distaste as well, giving E!"s mini-cam for manicures the finger.

In other instances, reporters have been the ones initiating change by asking male celebrities sexist questions, making for interesting responses and a developed awareness. Internet news site BuzzFeed hilariously called out the kinds of banal questions women are asked on the red carpet by posing them to male stars like Kevin Spacey, Eddie Redmayne, and Michael Keaton. Questions included: "How long did it take you to get ready?" "Can you give us a twirl?" and perhaps most comically "Are you wearing Spanx?"

With the "Me" generation, our actions influence the media; in turn, the media can reach greater audiences and serve as a proponent for change that once again filters back to the general population. The ebb and flow between the masses and media, and how the masses can authorize what they want the media to reflect is an indomitable turning point for Millennials, especially in the age of social media.

The resurgence of feminism isn't solely linked to the support of celebrity entertainers, however. Another global figure that is believed to have helped propel the movement is Barack Obama. Thanks to the 2012 elections, Obama running for presidency may have revived the fervor for the feminist movement. According to *The Feminist Factor* by Eleanor Smeal, published in Ms. Magazine, "...voters' views on feminism correlated with their choice of candidates. Among feminist women, some two-thirds (64%) voted for Obama, as did 54% of feminist-identified men. Looking at voters who identified as pro-choice, 61% cast their ballot for Obama."[18]

For this historic race, where the first Black American was elected President, minorities, as well as feminists, had a significant impact. Dubbed the "Feminist Factor," women were motivated to vote for Obama due to his testaments to nullify the War on Women. Obama, being a father of two daughters, was just what the country needed when looking to identify with a feminist role model who was also a father figure.

Historically, feminism has been a long-reigning movement with each generation pushing for a new amendment of women's right. So many people are now publically on board and in support of breaking the patriarchy. Having more people in the public limelight identify as feminists–one who supports equal social, political, and economic rights of the sexes–has been a major advancement during the epoch of Generation-Y.

Things Women were Discouraged from Doing in 2014

America, Europe, Iran, African countries, and India are just a few locations that have made headlines for their anti-women legislation, either furthering the disparity between men and women on the educational or working front, or suppressing women by regulating dress code or the rights they have to make decisions about their own bodies.

With help from Maureen Shaw's wildly viral list on Mic.com, the following is a rundown of 16 things women were prohibited from doing in just the year 2014:

1) February 19, 2014: President Museveni of Uganda signed a bill into law, prohibiting women from wearing mini-skirts, citing indecent exposure under the anti-pornography act.[19]

2) July 29, 2014: In Turkey, Deputy Prime Minister Bulent Arinc sought to prohibit laughter in public, believing mirth is the same as moral corruption.[20]

3) October 2014: Michigan schools ban young women from wearing yoga pants or leggings.[21]

4) June 2014: Iranian women were banned from watching the World Cup, or any sports, due to a divisive revolution in 1979.[22]

5) June 2014: In a 5-4 ruling for the Burwell vs Hobby Lobby case, the Supreme Court ruled family-owned corporations are exempt from covering birth control under the Affordable Healthcare Act (Viagra is still covered).[23]

6) July 2014: European Court of Human Rights banned the wearing of burqas and niqabs, reasoning that such prohibitions were to "protect gender equality."[24]

7) January 2014: BBC executives banned children's television presenters from wearing red lipstick, so as not to be a bad influence on young viewership.[25]

8) August 2014: Iranian women were prohibited from working as waitresses in public cafés and teahouses.[26]

9) October 2014: The CEO of Microsoft, Satya Nadella, discouraged women from asking for raises. He later apologized, stating his intended message was that women should not have to ask for raises to accommodate the gap in pay wages, but should, instead, trust the system.[27]

10) October 2014: Identifying and confronting male privilege is still risky, as noted by a woman commentator who responded to Jessica Williams' somewhat satirical video on The Daily Show. Jessica and most women in America are confronted daily by catcalls from men. Catcalling, or the unpleasant greetings, attempted banter, and provocative comments

made by male passersby, happens at all hours of the day, despite what the woman is wearing, and especially if a woman shows disinterest.

Jessica Williams made a comical video of her experiences (comical in the sense that she wanted this video to be educational and easy for both men and women to consume), noting that no matter which direction she went in to walk to work—"Four blocks north, three blocks west," and also "avoid the Wallstreet douches"—she was going to be harassed by men. A woman commenting on this video remarked that calling out this male privilege could incite or inflame the situation further.[28]

11) August 2014: Women from Pakistan, Bangladesh, Myanmar, and Chad who currently reside in Saudi Arabia are prohibited from marrying Saudi Arabian men. Current policy, in accordance with Islamic law, allows men to take up to four wives. The new toughened legislation is speculated to be, in part, a reactionary response to the influx of foreigners who live and make up the population of Saudi Arabia.[29]

12) April 2014: In America, body image and talks of weight are polarizing conversations. Of course, being healthy is the most important. However, when Brooke Birmingham incredibly shed 170 pounds and shared her story with *Shape* magazine, along with before and after photos, the publication shunned her post-weight-

loss body. Brooke had loose skin around her midsection, a normal occurrence after losing a drastic amount of weight, and *Shape* wanted Brooke to cover this up.

As a result, Brooke pulled her story and decided to publish it on her own blog instead, proudly showcasing her figure. The photo went viral across online platforms, reinforcing the "I am woman, hear me roar" proclamation that so many Millennials proudly champion.[30]

13) July 2014: The International eSports Federation (IeSF) poorly attempted to segregate gamers and competitors by gender. During that summer, policy was revealed that female video game players were banned from competing in *Hearthstone*. This gender-specific decree sparked ire amongst gamers and the general masses. The IeSF quickly reversed their gender-biased prohibition. [31]

14) March 2014: Eight-year-old Sunnie Kahle was harshly reprimanded at her Christian school for not fitting into the society-defined role of femininity. Her tomboy behavior was rebuked, with the school reaching out to her grandparents, stating, "…understand that God has made her female." Because she behaved too much like a boy, having a cropped haircut, wearing jeans, and showing an adoration for playing sports, the principal penned an uncomfortable letter to her grandparents.

Out of support for her, they later removed her from the school and placed Sunnie in a public institution.[32]

15) May 2014: The Navy confronted hospital corpsman, Jessica Sims, about the braided hairstyle that she had been wearing for a decade. The neatly braided bun fell into the category of "unauthorized" hair, as did most hairstyles commonly donned by Black American women.

For this reason, Sims believed this was a race-related issue, protesting that the ban of many of these coiffures included styles that worked with the natural texture of hair that Black women have. Chuck Hagel, Secretary of Defense, recognized the absurdity of the claim, and, after a three-month review of Sims' case, set a precedent to relax these hair regulations across military branches.[33]

16) January 2014: A Victoria's Secret associate prohibited a mother from breastfeeding her son in a fitting room area. Ashley Clawson, mom of two, politely asked to breastfeed her son in a fitting room, while a cashier checked out her purchases. Another store clerk chimed in, stating that Clawson should use the neighboring alleyway. She further encouraged the mother by saying that, because the alley was long, no one would see her if she breastfed her son at the end of the pathway. Ashley Clawson felt humiliated, especially in a place like Victoria's Secret. Victoria's Secret representatives

publically apologized, citing that they permit breastfeeding in their stores.[34]

9

Give It To Me Straight

Truth Bomb:

Heterosexual and cisgender privilege allows for many of us to participate in contemporary society without the fear of harassment or assault. We can publically express affection for our romantic partner un-threatened, subscribe to any religious denomination, and not have to worry about being terminated from our jobs (in over half of the states being gay is an actual, fire-able offense). If you end up in an emergency room, you know will not be denied medical attention because of who you are.

—

Pursuit of Inclusivity for the "Other"

Many Gen-Yers love to celebrate identity inclusivity. Though our views evoke divisive, emotional discourse with and among those who have socially conservative views, we are more in tune with what being an "other" feels like. As the most racially diverse generation in history, it is more likely that we are familiar with, afraid of, or have experienced instances of injustice, whether as a result of our race or cultural background. Even our class or economic status impacts how we're viewed in society. Because of our personal experiences, our empathy or even understanding of cultural disenfranchisement often easily extends to the LGBT+ community.

Millennials persistently pursue progress even when there's pushback. There are some Gen-Yers influenced by lifestyle or traditional family values that tie into religion or politics who do not share similar ideas of what equality means. However, for most Millennials, those who are in opposition are fading into the minority themselves. As of 2013, for example, 70% of Millennials were cited to believe that LGBT men and women deserve social equality.[1] Our tolerance levels are shifting as we continuously work to overturn systemic prejudices.

A main area that we're tackling, for example, is media representation. I now recognize more uproar for diversity in film and television than in previous years. This includes Kerry Washington's monumental 2015 speech at the GLAAD media awards, where she demonstrated fervor for gay rights and inclusivity to be present on television and in the entertainment industry in general. "We need more LGBT representation in the media. We need more LGBT characters and more LGBT storytelling. We need more diverse LGBT representation and by that, I mean lots of kinds of different kinds of LGBT people, living all kinds of lives, and this is big—we need more employment of LGBT people in front of and behind the camera!" she states, just as powerfully as her character Olivia Pope on *Scandal* would.

People in our neighborhoods, schools, workplaces, and even the public figures we interact with daily through media channels are integrating as we learn to accept and embrace different cultures. Subcultures, who were previously outcasts, are becoming part of the quotidian on screen and in real life, as Millennials continue to push for greater changes. The once standardized white-male, blond, blue-eyed, heterosexual, Christian image of America is being widened to accommodate and include minority groups.

To put things into perspective, I am a Millennial who is part of two sub-groups—one as an African-American and another as a woman. These traits reflect that I am a minority. I also fit into several groups of privilege. I am an able-bodied, middle-class Christian American. When it comes to not being White or male, I can handle that. I can cope with obstacles related to my minority status, like being called 'nigger' or dealing with harassment from men. Social justice issues that deal with LGBT+ rights are something that I do not live with daily. They may seem a little more nebulous, as I am removed from the prejudices that come along with being queer. However, my own "otherness" allows me the capacity to empathize.

Sometimes, however, the challenge comes when I get to step into my privilege of ignorance. I try to steer clear of this trap as often as I can. I may not experience the negative slurs, bullying, distasteful looks, hate crimes, and the fear of being rejected by friends and family that comes with being gay, bisexual, lesbian, or transgender, but I can offer support where needed as an ally.

Another common pain point that stirs up controversy surrounding LGBT+ inclusivity goes back to religion versus social equality. When growing up in a religious world that communicates a certain set of guidelines for how to live, we can be socialized to believe one thing over another. Man versus Deity, or Man versus Manmade Deity always conflict. This was the case with my family and me, and our values, until we learned otherwise. I know I am not the only one who has struggled with how religion can influence ideals about personal liberties. Now, I simply fear judgment for my LGBT+ friends, and know that my silence can perpetuate more violence and hate while playing into the identity-shaming philosophy of being closeted.

What makes Millennials a unique generation compared to our predecessors, however, is that our yearning for social equality typically trumps tradition even religious convention. Our own experiences in the "other" category as either non-white, non-male, or non-Christian has significant impact on our belief systems. When it comes to gender identity specifically, Gen-Yers most likely will witness someone close to us go through an experience that breaks that person's stamina or will to live, an experience that makes them feel shameful and guilty, or a negative view that will trigger a physical attack, execution, or hate crime.

Changing the Standard from Heteronormalcy to Inclusivity

Prejudices work hand in hand with fears. I remember my mother telling me once, "Being Black means we're lowering the property value in this neighborhood." We were, and still are, the others. Having this insight is painful. With socialized insecurities and fears, overanalyzing situations to make sure to compensate for my otherness becomes easy. The same prejudicial sentiment that comes with my mother's truth bomb can be applied to people who are lesbian, gay, bisexual, or transgender.

Just like my fears can stir up a chain reaction of insecurities and identity-questioning behaviors, so can a society's. A cultural fear of breaking uniformity means a population less able to be controlled and standardized by media, religion, and politics. With a diversified population follows a rearrangement of the pecking order, in every aspect of the quotidian lifestyle.

When it comes down to it, an idea of what normalcy embodies is governed by mass appeal, with the intent to generate profit and subdue change. To shape a culture's value systems, a recognizable, standardized image of what someone must personify is passed down through generations. This isolates minorities into sub-groups, pitting each person with a difference against the next individual with a difference. A prototype when it comes to sexuality and gender identity heavily relies on the cisgender image, male-female dyad. Those who do not fit this mold were, and still are, encouraged to adapt or hide.

Culturally, we are socialized as consumers or encouraged through organized politics and religion to favor heterosexual identities. We are very much systematically trained to snub anything that differs from what has been taught to have mass appeal. Therefore, the process of adaptation or trying to assimilate for those living as the "other" can be emotionally costly and shaming. Predominant in Millennial culture, however, has been the adamancy to oppose these superfluous ideas of societal uniformity, especially when it comes to sexuality and being open to love whomever a person happens to and is meant to love.

The shift in Western culture to include fluidity and diversification has admittedly been glacial. The 1969 Stonewall Inn riots in New York opened a much-needed reevaluation of LGBT+ rights at a time when those discussions were closeted in and of themselves. A steady stream of uprisings since then, both on the streets and in the media now ignites more tolerance and acceptance toward those who have sexual identities other than hetero-normalization. Generation-Y and equality proponents from the Gen-X, as well as Baby Boomer generation passionately work to establish a new normal that is inclusive of every sexual identity and orientation.

Over the past couple of decades, people have felt increasingly comfortable coming out, which is one reason why Gen-Y is credited as the most openly gay generation. Public figures like singers and musicians, actors and actresses, as well as politicians, have openly revealed their sexual orientation, while others have identified as an ally. There is now a larger community of lesbian, gay, bisexual, and transgender people, ranging from youth to adults that express liberation about their sexual orientation and identity.

This larger network of support does a few things: It allows for discussions and learning opportunities about the queer and transgender community to take place, encourages friends or family members of a person who has identified as LGBT+ to be more open and tolerant, and gradually builds acceptance, slowly devaluing induced stereotypes.

As more people openly identify as queer, Millennials progressively work to reduce stigma associated with non-heteronormative culture and communities. Barack Obama, who has been instrumental in enacting social reform during his presidency, declared support for LGBT+ rights in his 2012 State of the Union Address, even though his stance wavered at first. During his 2008 campaign, he was not in favor of same-sex marriage. However, he shifted views stating, "At a certain point, I've just concluded that for me, personally, it is important for me to go ahead and affirm that I think same-sex couples should be able to get married." The Human Rights Campaign reported that this was the first time terms such as "bisexual" and "transgender" were used in a State of the Union Address.[2]

Current strides to establish and cement LGBT+ rights have been full force. What was once almost uniformly thought of as a sort of disorder, or epidemic that could be fixed by religious rehabilitation, similar to the experience Megan's character faced in the 1999 cult classic *But I'm a Cheerleader,* is more accepted and better understood. Unfortunately, powering change often comes at a price.

Transgender 17-year-old Leelah Alcorn, for example, took her life, crediting her parents' rejection of her and her identity as the reason. She was forced to attend counseling sessions with "Christian therapists" who shamed her, stating that she was "selfish and wrong and that [she] should look to God for help." A worldwide petition launched, getting the attention of President Barack Obama and the White House Administration. Support was far reaching, with the White House stating, "As part of our dedication to protecting America's youth, this Administration supports efforts to ban the use of conversion therapy for minors."[3]

More and more religious therapy is frowned upon, yet there's still a larger issue that advocates struggle to address: LGBT+ youth homelessness. Combative relationships between a non-supportive parent and a child who identifies as queer can create a divisive dynamic, forcing the child to leave home. Between couch surfing, shelters, or surviving living on the streets, increased youth homelessness has trickled upward since the early 2000s.

In a combined research and report initiative with the Forty to None Project/True Colors Fund, The Palette Fund, and the Williams Institute, service agencies who work with LGBT+ youth who are at risk of becoming homeless were surveyed. Data shows that there was a 12% increase over a 10-year span in the number of LGBT+ youth respondents that housing agencies helped.[4] And there's the grim statistic, noted by Center for American Progress, that approximately 20-40% of the homeless youth population identify as LGBT, compared to only 5-10% of the overall youth population.

School dropout rates also reflect a non-tolerant climate, as bullying and harassment influences an adolescent's likeliness to complete their education. The same Center for American Progress study highlights that gay and transgender youth are two times less likely to finish high school or pursue a college degree, compared to the national average.[5] What's worse is institutionalized school and housing systems typically offer little to no support for queer youth.

As the "gayest" generation,[6] it's important for Gen-Yers to not only champion equal rights in areas such as the workplace or our social lives, but to advocate on behalf of those who are part of upcoming generations. The generation after us can benefit from our continued support and advocacy of equality in school systems, housing agencies, or even at home as in the case of Alcorn.

National Campaigns Inspire Social Movements & Change

Millennials are aware that attraction and sexual orientation exists on a spectrum, with no one being completely hetero- or homosexual. This still may be tough for some Baby Boomers or members of Gen-X to understand or even explain, especially parents. Parents raising a child who identifies as LGBT+ may even face prejudices and intolerance, which is why encouraging campaigns are disseminated across cities and social media channels.

Project ALY (Accept LGBT Youth), a bus campaign in central Brooklyn, targeted parents of queer youth, with the intention to change views and promote tolerance. National campaigns, such as *It Gets Better*, and organizations like The Trevor Project, have also worked hand-in-hand to educate the masses, while encouraging LGBT+ adolescents to remain hopeful through periods of harassment and bullying. Overall, the goal is that as others open up in regards to their sexual identity, especially youth, supportive communities will follow suit. Millennial influence has been significant in building this increasingly tolerant climate.

To give statistical support to Millennial impact, a 2013 Pew Research Center study found that in 2001, 57% of Americans did not support same-sex marriage while in 2014 that number dropped to 40%. Additional data also paints that narrative. In 2013, a staggering 70% of Millennials were on board with same-sex marriage, compared to 2003 when only 51% of Millennials were in support. As Millennials start to make up the majority of the adult population, numbers shift in favor of equal rights for all.

Prior generations have also started to shift their views, either coming to terms with the changing beliefs of the world, or relenting because they have a friend or family member who feels comfortable opening up about their identity.[7] Media director for the Human Rights Campaign, Michael Cole-Schwartz explains this greater slant toward equality stating, "The meta narrative is that we win these fights because Americans know that LGBT people are their neighbors, their cousins, their aunts and uncles, the people they sit next to in church, and the people they shop with at the grocery store."[8]

In 2007 I moved cross-country from Detroit, a city that at the time lacked racial diversity and tolerance for those who identified as LGBT+, to Southern California. Palm trees were just as magical as the different cultures I would see and experience in person, all taking up different views in my new landscape in a way that felt natural and beautiful.

When college started, I was assigned to live in one of the only dorms with gender-neutral bathrooms in a building for students enrolled in the progressive Johnston

Center for Integrative Studies program. No women- or men-only space existed, and inclusivity was the norm. Surrounded by peers who were knowledgeable on current social justice issues, the students in this program–which I would later join–celebrated being on the outskirts. They challenged topics that were controversial at the time, using their art, words, and insight. One of these issues included LGBT+ efforts.

I learned to quickly adjust to the new atmosphere, and though difficult to embrace at times, my college years helped carve out new views on LGBT+ social rights and equality.

The gender-neutral bathrooms became an important piece of the puzzle when it came to me understanding this community. LGBT+ students had a safe space to live and act freely in accordance with their identity, a privilege cisgender people commonly disregard. It was startling at first to witness men comfortable in women's clothing, and women who altered their appearance to resemble men at ease with their appearance. I brought to the table the only experience I had: I had never seen a person who was transgender in waking life, only on television. Of course, I know how dangerous and how many self-imposed boundaries and prejudgments this can create, as I often hear that phrase directed at me when people say, "I've only ever seen a Black person on TV." Knowing that the media relies on tropes and stereotypes to succeed at mainstreaming an idea, I had fallen prey to these social constructs and had to readjust in college.

My experiences in this dorm helped me learn how to empathize with students and professors alike who are LGBT+. One colleague even shared how his parents no longer supported or accepted him, a battle that continued for the four years that I got to know him. I even shared in the celebration of two same-sex students marrying. What I ultimately learned was how something as seemingly simple as having gender-neutral bathrooms that provides an environment for inclusivity, quickly leads to more acceptance and peer-to-peer connection. It establishes a space where people can simultaneously learn from each other while feeling safe.

Having restrooms designated for men and women is another privilege of the cisgender, leaving people who do not identify as one of the two binary genders out of the picture. Luckily for me, my dorm was progressive on this issue before this topic even ventured into the mainstream. Student-led efforts to have gender-neutral bathrooms started as early as the '70s on the campus I attended, and campus legislation made the efforts official in the '90s. Fast forward to 2009, and heated debates over gender-neutral bathrooms had already reached the ears of the public.

One of the first campaigns to achieve nationwide publicity included efforts from 16-year-old Kyle Giard-Chase, who had advocated for inclusive public restrooms at the South Burlington High School in Vermont. Two years prior, in 2007, the University of Vermont invested around $10,000 to build four gender-neutral restrooms for transgender students, citing the necessity for inclusion and accessibility.[9] Now that LGBT+ concerns are more visible to the public, efforts from supporters are ramping up to improve quality of life. On April 8, 2015, the White House, for example, opened doors to their first gender-neutral restroom, coinciding with Obama's executive orders to protect federal employees from discrimination.[10]

Peer-to-Peer Connections & Celebrity Involvement Draw in Greater LGBT+ Support

The push for national support has been getting a boost from online peer-to-peer connection thanks to social sharing platforms Facebook, Twitter and Instagram. Generation-Y has cultivated national support for LGBT+ equality, using Web networking to influence our social media circles. In fact, our relationship with social media is so interpedently linked with activists' efforts that we are comfortable sharing personal stories, political stances on polarizing issues, and even check-ins if we're participating in a citywide protest, all by way of status updates. Bloggers are even more in demand for larger news sites, including *The Huffington Post*, where confessional-style narratives drive public support and attention.

Thinking back to late March of 2013, specifically March 26, Facebook was alight with users changing their profile picture to the pink-on-red equal sign, soon-to-be emblematic for same-sex equality. The trend was urged by the Human Rights Campaign (HRC) as the U.S. Supreme Court met to discuss the future of same-sex marriage. What started as a post from the HRC encouraging those to change their Facebook profile image led to a surplus of 2.7 million people updating their profile image by the following day, noted by researcher Eytan Bakshy in his visual report as part of the Facebook Data Science Team.[11]

What was once ridiculed as Slacktivism, or activism through social media efforts, proved to be far-reaching as online users were able to express solidarity cross-country in fewer than 24 hours. The wildfire dissemination of the Facebook image update may not have directly affected legislation, but indirectly it can be said to have had a profound impact on our social justice views.

As Melanie Tannenbaum wrote in her essay on the topic of Facebook and marriage equality for SCIENTIFIC AMERICAN™, people are more likely to follow along with what's deemed as *prescriptive* norms versus *descriptive* norms. Descriptive norms outline what a person should do. For example, the statement *you should support marriage equality* is a descriptive norm. A prescriptive norm showcases what everyone is already doing. The case of social users changing their profile image in favor of same-sex rights is an example of this. What this does is create a climate where people do not want to feel left out. With Facebook being a platform where beliefs are constantly deluged in newsfeeds, those who do not have similar beliefs or who choose not to publically share their beliefs stick out in social crowds.[12]

Millennials are the generation that has spearheaded this reliance on the Internet for the transfer and distribution of information. With Facebook, Twitter, and Instagram, social and political beliefs can reach international media outlets in a matter of hours. Courtesy of the social-network effect, Millennials report to the World Wide Web to respond 24/7 with personal stories. This makes rallying together and finding liked-minded allies easier, while allowing audiences to instantaneously gauge where popular opinion falls.

Through the Web, we've heard stories of hate crimes, gay and transgender youth who have committed suicide, unwarranted harassment and bullying, and unnecessary religious intervention. We've launched petitions sparking legislation reform in response, we've started national campaigns, and we've created an urgency to mandate change. Overall, support continues to increase as these stories surface, oftentimes from firsthand experiences. And thanks to peer-to-peer networking, celebrities and brands are also taking notice, participating in measures of reform.

Millennials' stance on LGBT+ rights, as well as the views of celebrity activists, has coincided, driving exponential awareness. As far as contemporary media representation, Ellen DeGeneres has galvanized mass support for queer people, normalizing LGBT+ culture for middle-market America. She has reached the housewives' demographic, as well as youth. Additionally, she has set cultural touchstones for equality, both as a political and cultural figure. When she came out in 1997 on her sitcom, a year after the Defense of Marriage Act (DOMA) was enacted, she lost endorsements and even appeal, but was solidified as a political activist who would later become eponymous with same-sex equality.

Gen-Yers who have followed in DeGeneres' footsteps, either as a hallmark for the LGBT+ movement or as an ally, include transgender American actress, Laverne Cox; singer, musician, and entertainer, Lady Gaga; and Andreja Pejić, the first transgender model to be featured in *Vogue*. Other national and international public figures, who may not be categorized as Millennials, but who still have revolutionized same-sex equality includes Jason Collins, the first athlete to come out as gay; Anderson Cooper, journalist and TV personality; and Caitlyn Jenner who announced her identity as a transgender woman in the spring of 2015.

The inequality gap is shrinking, creating new opportunities for succeeding generations, including transgender 14-year-old Jazz Jennings. She was hired to participate in Johnson and Johnson's #SeeTheRealMe campaign for skincare line Clean & Clear.[13] This monumental moment is similar to when Ellen DeGeneres became a commercial model for international brand CoverGirl in September 2008.

So here's where we are at with LGBT+ rights: The Supreme Court ruling in *Obergefell v. Hodges* now grants same-sex marriage as legal in all states, citing state-wide bans on same-sex marriage as unconstitutional.[14] This legislation passed in June 2015 (Massachusetts was the first state to support marriage equality in 2004). The first LGBT+-friendly national sorority, Gamma Rho Lambda, has opened its doors at the University of Texas, providing queer-focused support and inclusivity. Representation of those who identify as queer is now more present and active in popular culture, with shows like *Glee* addressing LGBT+ issues in a high school environment. Even prolific author J.K. Rowling clarified that supporting character Dumbledore in her mega-successful series *Harry Potter* was indeed gay.

What Each Initial Stands for in
LGBTTQQIAAP Acronym

Lesbian – A woman who is sexually or romantically attracted to another woman.

Gay – A blanket term primarily used to describe those who identify as homosexual, whether they are a man or woman.

Bisexual – A person who is sexually or romantically attracted to both men and women.

Transgender – A person whose identity does not correspond with the biological male or female gender they were given at birth.

Transsexual – A person who physically alters their body, typically through surgical procedures or hormone treatment, to reflect the gender that they identify with.

Queer – Similar to the term *Gay,* queer is an all-encompassing term used to represent a person who does not subscribe to conventional gender identifications or norms.

Questioning – A person who is in the process of exploring their own sexual identity and orientation.

Intersex – A person born with sexual anatomy that does not match with either gender identity of male or female.

Asexual – A person who does not experience sexual attraction to any group of people.

Ally – A straight person who advocates and supports people who are queer.

Pansexual – A person who is sexually or romantically attracted to a person, regardless of biological sex, gender identity, or gender expression.

10

Myth of the Post-Racial Society

Truth Bomb:

The official #BlackLivesMatter Organization was founded by Patrisse Cullors, Opal Tometi, and Alicia Garza in response to the 2012 murder of unarmed Black teenager, Trayvon Martin, by White civilian, George Zimmerman.

Zimmerman was found not guilty of the murder, causing protests to erupt both online and offline. #BlackLivesMatter was used to encapsulate the collective anger felt around the world.

The hashtag continues to trend when a civilian's race is suspected to be the reason for excessive, unneeded, and violent action as punitive measure, such as when a Black American is unjustly killed by a police officer. When no action is taken against law enforcement for perpetrating a violent crime against a minority, the hashtag re-emerges.

#BlackLivesMatter should not be used in conjunction with #AllLivesMatter. In fact, activists have made a point to de-emphasize the latter. #AllLivesMatter devalues the significance a person's skin color can have in making them a target for unwanted and unnecessary violence. While recognizing that every life is significant, the #BlackLivesMatter movement aims to specifically acknowledge the disproportionate rates at which minorities are unfairly brutalized and cruelly outcast in society.

—

American Pride and Prejudice

I remember reading an article about modern Black American parents who attempted to shelter their three children from systemic and episodic racism. Their efforts failed them. One day as their son was peacefully strolling home, a car pulled up beside him with the passenger carefully poking his head out to address the teen as "nigger."

The father, who shared this story in an essay, went on to say how his 15-year-old son now feared walking alone and was cautious of vehicles that seemed to slow in an approaching manner.[1] While teens who are White Americans, or who fall into the category of being a festishized minority (e.g. a person with a racial blend or ethnicity that has desirable features comparable to standards of contemporary media. Festishized minorities often have a fair complexion and others typically are unable to tell what race, ethnicity, or nationality they identify with) are concerned or aware of racism, Black Americans have to grow up living and coping with it daily.

For example, I commonly face what's called microagressions, or everyday slights, insults, remarks or behaviors that tend to be derogatory in nature (regardless of intention), which are targeted toward people of color. This occurs when peers call me their "token Black friend" or curiously prod at my unnaturally straight, relaxed hair, questioning if it's real. Sometimes I'll even get remarks inspired by television tropes asking if I eat watermelon regularly or if I can teach friends how to "twerk." Though made in jest, these microagressions demean and devalue, and ultimately end up being hurtful. These are subtle instances of indirect racism. More direct forms of intolerance include harassment, as experienced by the 15-year old boy mentioned earlier. This, too, is something I would come to encounter and deal with.

It was around the holiday season and I was driving to meet with a friend. Our mild winter weather was more spring-like; even at night our chill lacked bluster. I navigated a winding freeway exit ramp, pausing before merging into the next lane. A little too slow to regain speed, an impatient driver fired a series of loud honks before angrily passing me. About a mile down the road, we ended up adjacent to each other at a red light.

He rolled down his window, mine already cracked, and yelled "nigger!" I could hear both the venom and jocularity in his voice. He wanted to taunt me before speeding off, hastily making a left turn into the night. The 15-year-old boy's experience that I had read about was now my own.

On the drive back, I started to question how many White Americans felt a sense of superiority with the ability to emotionally, socially, and mentally oppress a minority with one single word. My mom chuckled uneasily when I told her, recalling her own past being born in the racially turbulent and violent 60s, which isn't too different from today.

Many Millennials still have trouble acknowledging that racism exists and adopt the notion that we are now a "colorblind" society that does not focus on race. Although the majority of people agree that racism has decreased toward Black Americans in the past 60 years, White Americans are more likely to believe that racism or discrimination has ended completely toward people of color. Black Americans and Latinos insist that inequalities are still part of day-to-day living. What is more interesting is that reports show some White Americans believe they are targets of discrimination themselves, more so than minorities. This is referred to as reverse racism.

Researchers from Tufts and Harvard document this shift in perspective in the report "Whites See Racism as a Zero-Sum Game That They Are Now Losing." White Americans are now starting to believe they are the main victims of racial bias and discrimination. The research conducted by Samuel R. Sommers and Michael I. Norton leads us to ask how and when did we form a skewed perception of racial progress and why is it an issue?[2]

Racial-Bias, Social Media, & White Privilege

The day is November 4, 2008. Exhilaration, hostility, and trepidation are rampantly flooding the globe, and in America, millions sit on edge. Black American Democratic nominee, Barack Obama, faces off against Republican John McCain for the United States presidency.

Votes are being tallied and results are whooshing in, lighting up on screen, with various news anchors from each major network announcing the candidate who had which state or region. Where I'm situated, everything is happening in the lobby of my dorm, almost 100 of us, students, staff, and faculty piled into an old-fashioned space with wall-to-wall wood paneling. A projector fed us second-by-second updates on the presidential race.

By 11:00pm EST, America had had a victor. Obama, the first Black American to win the presidency, overtook McCain, with 53% versus 46% of the popular vote. With a collective feeling of jubilation sweeping nationwide, for not only Democrats, but for minorities, history had been made.

Having a Black American occupy, arguably the most powerful position in the world, shifted how we view race, but not quite for the better. The stumbling block that followed Obama's presidency was the belief that we are now living in a post-racial society. Remarks from conservative pundit William Bennett stating, "You don't take any excuses anymore from anybody who says, 'The deck is stacked'" after Obama won the election evoked this sentiment.[3]

To some, racism seems to have ended with the start of Obama's presidency. Sadly this isn't the case. Race-related tension in America after Obama's presidency isn't simmering, it's boiling over and sparking this generation's civil rights movement bringing to light the modern day Black-White divide....

I remember once, my mom sharing with me the memory of when a store clerk refused to serve her and my grandmother in the late '60s because she was Black. My grandmother could easily (and for a while, I would have used the adjective "enviably") pass as a White American.

She was always proud to be a Black woman, however, and never considered herself to be anything but. One day, while my grandmother and mom shopped, my mom being around six years old, my grandmother encountered a store clerk. At the moment, my mother had run off to retrieve something so it was just the store clerk and my grandmother interacting. When my mom returned, and the store clerk realized my grand-mother, the woman she was assisting all along, had a Black child, she refused any help or service going forward. Unfortunately, similar to the story above, profiling still exists in modern American society.

Five plus decades after my mother and grandmother's incident with racial profiling, Black Americans continue to face instances where they are targeted, followed, and harassed while shopping. Millennial Trayon Christian, a 19-year-old at the time when he was unjustly cuffed, was held and questioned after purchasing a $350 belt from a luxury department store.

An engineering student who worked part-time, Christian saved money to buy a designer Ferragamo belt. He presented adequate identification to the cashier and paid using his debit card. After leaving the store, he was confronted by undercover officers who arrested him and later questioned how Christian could afford such an expensive purchase. He stated that his identification card was real to combat converse allegations, and officers later verified that he was telling the truth. Afterwards Christian was interviewed and he stated, "Why me? I guess because I'm a young black man, and you know, people do a credit card scam, so they probably thought that I was one of them."[4]

The above is an obvious example of racial profiling and Millennials understand this to be unjust and racist. Where tracking discriminatory behavior becomes tricky is when we don't realize we are contributing to the greater problem through seemingly small acts.

While people may believe that everyone is treated equally and most importantly, that *we* treat others equally, we often perpetuate racism unknowingly. By donning blackface, throwing a culturally themed party unrelated to our heritage that plays up harmful tropes (i.e. a Spanish-themed party with stick-on mustaches, plastic maracas, sombreros, etc.), or not filtering comments when communicating with someone different from us, we reinforce race-related biases and behaviors.

Fortunately, technology, the Web, and social media are used by Millennials to point out these acts of discrimination, intentional or otherwise. A lot of us are receptive to the messaging and pass along educational tidbits as well as personal stories. Popular websites like BuzzFeed produce listicles such as "21 Racial Micro-aggressions You Hear on a Daily Basis" or videos like "If Black People Said the Stuff White People Say (This is What it Would Be Like...)" to help us discern racial biases and self-reflect on our interaction with other cultures. They also help get the word out relatively quickly. Another perk of social media and Web communication includes the ability to document racism as it happens as veritable proof that it persists.

Early in 2015, two fraternity members at the University of Oklahoma were caught on camera singing an upsetting chant that highlighted Black Americans not being able to pledge Sigma Alpha Epsilon. Lines from the chant include, "There will never be a nigger in SAE. There will never be a nigger in SAE. You can hang him from a tree, but he can never sign with me. There will never be a nigger in SAE." The video broadcasted on social media channels, causing protests across the country to erupt; both the university and fraternity took immediate punitive action. The two members videoed were expelled from the University of Oklahoma, and the fraternity Sigma Alpha Epsilon launched a national investigation to determine where the chant originated.[5]

Other headlining news like the killings of Trayvon Martin, Renisha Mcbride, Freddie Gray, Eric Garner, and Tamir Rice, among others, or the unjust police brutality brought on by New York's controversial Stop and Frisk program that encouraged racial profiling by law enforcement,[6] drew worldwide attention because of social media.

In 2011, for example, a mixed race, 17-year-old teen named Alvin documented his unjust encounter with police officers in Harlem using his iPod to secretly record the hostile stop-and-frisk interaction. He was stopped simply for looking suspicious. In the recording you can hear the teen asking, "Why did you push me like that for?" to which an officer irately responds "Shut your fuckin' mouth before I slap you." The video was uploaded to news site Upworthy in 2013 and then further shared across the web.

We have social platforms to document and capture these instances as proof that these events really happen. Thus, when we continue to assert that we are living in a post-racial society in spite of these events we take away from the progress fought for, including the support, understanding, and empathy garnered for victims of discrimination.

Acknowledging that the U.S. was founded on principles of racial inequality is easy. Recognizing that the issue persists remains a challenge for some. The racial divide between Black and White Americans may be blurred compared to the past, but one way we know it survives is through systemic oppression. This includes wealth disparity, unequal education through lack of funding, and residential segregation as only a few disadvantages Black Americans and people of color experience.

According to 2010 Federal Reserve data, White Americans held 88.4% of the nation's wealth, while Black Americans held only 2.7%.[7] The wealth disparity ties into the type of education students of color have access to. The Center for American Progress published a report titled "Unequal Education, Federal Loophole Enables Lower Spending on Students of Color," underlining how publically funded education shortchanges non-white, minority youth.[8] I was one of those students.

At the age of 11, I and about 100 other students went to take an entrance exam for one of the few private middle schools in Detroit. Our testing centers frequently lacked heat in the dead of winter, but, at this age, we thought this was normal. Winding through narrow, unlit halls in a dilapidated building, we found our way to a common room where would be administered exams.

Our gloves covered our trembling fingers as we tried to complete Scantron test forms. How could we ever prove that we were intellectually worthy, when the educational system didn't have enough faith in us to provide us with heat or financially set up our school system to succeed? Later, we would bitterly discover that suburban schools in the area would have the basics such as heat, as well as luxuries like fully stocked libraries, working computers, modernized testing facilities, and other amenities to ensure educational needs were met.

Why is this significant? We know that schools in impoverished neighborhoods have a higher rate of crime and violence. This can ultimately interfere with learning and the ability for students to get an education in a safe environment. We also know that with fewer resources, the ability to develop key skills diminishes. Without the proper space for learning, minority youth are less likely to receive a strong education and are funneled back into society set up for failure.

Though proof exists that minorities face a severe disadvantage economically and socially, getting this information across in a way that encourages productive progress is difficult. We can start, however, by examining how historical events have had an effect on modern-day Black American culture and use this knowledge to work to create an even playing field for minorities.

A tall brick-and-mortar location established as the Freedman's Savings and Trust headquarters stuck out on Pennsylvania Avenue in Washington, D.C. With 19 buildings by 1867 spread across the south, as well as the former headquarters in New York, this building, as well as the others, would be a place where Black Americans could start a savings account. This was going to alleviate the extreme socio-economic gap between newly emancipated slaves and White Americans.

Nearly a decade later, however, the promise of establishing financial equality was lost. Freedman's shut its doors permanently in 1874, the downfall speculated to be caused by questionable investments used with the money Black Americans entrusted to the financial institution. Thousands of Black Americans realized they would never be able to regain their lost savings, which was often the only money they had.

As we talk about the current wealth gap, it's important to look to the past and examine why and how things occurred. White Americans typically come into their wealth through inheritance, which explains why they hold a majority of the nation's wealth. Black Americans lack this inner-generational financial stability and are unable to maintain the same status economically due in part to events like the Freedman's debacle.[9]

Residential segregation traces back to the Civil War era, as well. Lenders during that time were hesitant to provide loans to Black Americans to prevent property acquirement. If able to secure a loan, they often came with unfair interest rates that priced minorities out of the market. White Americans were not financially restricted and had the advantage to obtain more land at lower rates.[10]

Although Black Americans in contemporary society can purchase property freely, this freedom comes at a cost. In their 2006 executive summary, The Center for Responsible Lending notes that Black Americans were

"30% more likely to receive a higher-rate loan than White borrowers, even after accounting for differences in risk."[11] In Brave New Film's *Racism is Real* video we learn that "Black clients are shown 17.7% fewer houses for sale."[12] Because of residential segregation and the wealth disparity that trickled down generationally, minorities are often locked into impoverished neighborhoods with little to no resources, including funding for education, or in the case of Flint, Michigan, clean drinking water.

Navigating race-related issues can be complicated and some resist the idea of racial bias all together. In the essay *Checking My Privilege: Character As the Basis of Privilege* written by Tal Fortgang, Fortgang asserts that "White privilege" is not a determining factor for one's success. He rules out discriminatory bias in regards to gender, race, and nationality. While Fortgang does not want to identify as a person who enjoys the benefits that come with White male privilege, recognizing that Black Americans experience drawbacks can establish a more truthful reality.

At the onset of the Millennium, the labor market stalled, a palpable side effect of the recession. An estimated 2.6 million jobs were lost in 2008,[13] and a feeling of desperation was ubiquitous. In order for American households to stay afloat and survive, people needed jobs.

But not everyone was receiving the same treatment when job-hunting and this became evident quickly.

Minorities started to realize that they were at a disadvantage. Applying for jobs was difficult, but securing preliminary steps, such as an interview, was especially tough for people of color. Even if Black Americans or non-White candidates possessed equivalent credentials or greater, they were overlooked. How was this possible? It was all in the name and, in some cases, the identity built around where a degree was obtained.

Take José Zamora: he applied for hundreds of jobs that he knew he was qualified for with no callbacks. Day after day, week after week, month after month he would submit his résumé in hopes of landing a position. He knew the market was tough, but to not make it to the interviewing stage with his qualifications surprised him. He then came up with the idea to eliminate a letter from his name to change his identity on paper. This worked. José became Joe, and he finally started to receive responses.[14]

Yvonne Orr, daughter of Blank Panthers members, faced a similar predicament. Removing any affiliation with historically black organizations from her résumé, including that she attended Hampton University, a famous Black educational institution, was painful. She was used to asserting herself as a proud woman of color. Orr admitted to *The New York Times*, "I wrestled with what kind of message I was sending to my children, in raising them to be very proud of who they are."[15] In the end, she decided to modify, or "Whiten," her résumé to be considered as a potential candidate for a job.

Additional stories, as well as experiments, circulated online about this phenomenon where a Black American or non-White American changed their name and/or race on a job application to bypass the initial screening process. In the end it worked, with some candidates even reapplying for jobs under their new identity and receiving a callback. Adopting a Eurocentric identity on paper provides the opportunity for minorities to overcome another obstacle in job-hunting. This is something that some White Americans, including Fortgang, overlook when discussing privilege.

Résumé consultant, Tammy Kabell gives further credence to this discriminatory behavior when hiring, telling NBC News, "I've had frank discussions with HR managers and hiring managers in the corporate world, and they tell me when they see a name that's ethnic or a Black name, they perceive that person as having low education or coming from a lower socioeconomic class."[16]

What this shows is that even though some believe we are living in a society where race no longer matters, or that we're colorblind, one's identity absolutely has an effect on the opportunities that we're given and the biased circumstances we have to regularly face.

Changing Perspectives Changes the Narrative

Black Americans come face to face with discriminatory acts of violence frequently. Most times in these situations there is a lopsided power dynamic, such as the profiling and, often, heinous killing of innocent Black men and women by law enforcement. Other times, violent actions stem from civilians. In these cases a debate arises questioning if a perpetrator of a violent act was reacting out of self-defense or if the reaction *was* racially motivated.

One act of domestic terrorism left little room for debate however, and made clear that racism remains a current national problem: the shooting rampage of Dylann Roof. His attack was followed with sadistic protests, including the burning of numerous Black churches in the south. That, combined with the dispute to remove the Confederate flag in all states, solidified that we are not living in the post-racial society that we thought we were.

When Dylann Roof entered a church one evening to massacre nine Black Americans during service, he went in prepared to start another Civil War. Some news pundits credited his behavior to mental illness at first, failing to recognize Roof's intentions. However, the discovery of his manifesto revealed what a great deal of the American population had already suspected: his actions were a racially motivated act of terrorism. What also came to light was that through an online community he participated in, other White Americans shared and supported his discriminatory beliefs and behavior.

The morning after the mass shooting occurred, I shared condolences as well as personal fears on Facebook. A friend of mine re-shared, noting that, as a White American woman, she finally understood racism is real. My reality finally made a little more sense to her.

Millennials contribute to accelerating progress in an effort to reach the post-racial society romanticized. We know how to document events with technology and make racial injustices public quickly. With support from entertainers, entertainment is changing as well to better and more accurately represent cultures, eliminating harmful tropes. Extraordinary writer Shonda Rhimes paints a normalized narrative for Black Americans on screen to chip away at conscious stereotypes that contribute to unconscious biases. And Amandla Stenberg, famous for her role as Rue in the popular *Hunger Games* film made a video pointing out instances of cultural appropriation in the industry that other stars have capitalized on.[17]

Even the 2015 Oscars received criticism for minimally spotlighting successful Black films, earning the annual awards show the title as "the Whitest Oscars since 1995." No person of color received a nomination that year. When this repeated for the 2016 Oscars, the hashtag #OscarsSoWhite reemerged and a firestorm of conversations ensued. People from all backgrounds vehemently protested the awards show, prompting the Board of Governors of the Academy of Motion Picture Arts to unanimously vote to include more diversified membership, with the goal to double the number of women and diverse members by the year 2020.

Though significant, more changes are needed to create a culture where racism is fully abolished. Bree Newsome, famous for courageously removing the South Carolina Confederate flag asks, "Is the United States prepared/willing to tackle White supremacy the same way it has gone after Islamic extremism? If not, why not?"[18] This question will continue to echo through generations until equality is established for all.

Today, I face the same fears of the 15-year-old Black American who was accosted by a White stranger. My surroundings, wherever I am, never feel safe. Walking alone at night in a hoodie calls to mind Trayvon Martin and when I window shop, I immediately approach a sales clerk with a friendly greeting so I'm not mistaken as a person casing their retail location. Even when I applied for jobs after being laid-off, I considered using a friend's photo as my LinkedIn picture to show that I was White instead of Black, a thought that occurred when submitting over 300 résumés only led to a handful of interviews. These fears of mine, and the fears of other minorities are not an outcome of a post-racial system, but a symptom of a nation still trying to iron out what racial equality means.

Unarmed Black Americans Killed by Law Enforcement from 1964-2015:

Racial profiling by law enforcement has led to the untimely deaths of numerous Black Americans. Many were either unarmed when they were killed, or struggled with a mental health issue.

Here is a compiled list of many of those killed by law enforcement from 1964-2015: [19][20]

2015: Matthew Ajibade (Savannah, GA)

2015: Brian Pickett (Los Angeles, CA)

2015: Andre Murphy, Sr. (Norfolk, NE)

2015: Artago Howard (Strong, AR)

2015: Alvin Haynes (San Francisco, CA)

2015: Jeremy Lett (Tallahassee, FL)

2015: Natasha McKenna (Fairfax, VA)

2015: Terry Price (Tulsa, OK)

2015: Calvon Reid (Coconut Creek, FL)

2015: Thomas Allen, Jr. (St Louis, MO)

2015: Charly 'Africa' Keunang (Los Angeles, CA)

2015: Darrell 'Hubbard' Gatewood (Oklahoma

City, OK)

2015: Tony Robinson (Madison, WI)

2015: Bernard Moore (Atlanta, GA)

2015: Anthony Hill (Chamblee, GA)

2015: Terrance Moxley (Mansfield, OH)

2015: Jonathan Paul (Arlington, TX)

2015: Askari Roberts (Rome, GA)

2015: Brandon Jones (Cleveland, OH)

2015: Denzel Brown (Bay Shore, NY)

2015: Dominick Wise (Culpeper, VA)

2015: Phillip White (Vineland, NJ)

2015: Donald 'Dontay' Ivy (Albany, NY)

2015: Eric Harris (Tulsa, OK)

2015: Walter Scott (North Charleston)

2015: Freddie Gray (Baltimore, MD)

2015: Frank 'Trey' Shephard III (Houston, TX)

2015: Darrell Brown (Hagerstown, MD)

2015: Norman Cooper (San Antonio, TX)

2015: William Chapman II (Portsmouth, VA)

2015: David Felix (New York, NY)

2015: Bryan Overstreet (Sylvester, GA)

2015: Brendon Glenn (Los Angeles, CA)

2015: Nuwnah Laroche (Ridgefield Park, NJ)

2015: Jason Champion, (Ridgefield Park, NJ)

2015: Sam Holmes (Fridley, MN)

2015: Lorenzo Hayes (Spokane, WA)

2015: Richard Davis (Rochester, NY)

2015: Ross Anthony (Dallas, TX)

2015: Alan Williams (Greenville, SC)

2015: Kris Jackson (South Lake Tahoe, CA)

2015: Jermaine Benjamin (Vero Beach, FL)

2015: Spencer McCain (Owings Mills, MD)

2015: Kevin Judson (McMinnville, OR)

2015: Jonathan Sanders (Stonewall, MS)

2015: Salvado Ellswood (Plantation, FL)

2015: Darrius Stewart (Memphis, TN)

2015: Samuel Dubose (Cincinnati, OH)

2015: Christian Taylor (Arlington, TX)

2015: Troy Robinson (Decatur, GA)

2015: Asshams Manley (District Heights, MD)

2015: Samuel Harrell (Beacon, NY)

2015: George Mann (Stone Mountain, GA)

2015: Felix Kumi (Mount Vernon, NY)

2015: India Kager (Virginia Beach, VA)

2015: Wayne Wheeler (Detroit, MI)

2015: Keith McLeod (Reisterstown, MD)

2015: Frank Smart (Pittsburgh, PA)

2015: Naeschylus Vinzant (Aurora, CO)

2015: Curtis Jordan (Huntsville, AL)

2015: Kevin Bajoie (Baton Rouge, LA)

2015: Albert Davis (Orlando, FL)

2015: James Carney III (Cincinnati, OH)

2015: Junior Prosper (North Miami, FL)

2015: Paterson Brown Jr. (Midlothian, VA)

2015: Rayshaun Cole (Chula Vista, CA)

2015: Anthony Ashford (San Diego, CA)

2015: Michael Marshall (Denver, CO)

2015: Jamar Clark (Minneapolis, MN)

2015: Nathaniel Pickett (Barstow, CA)

2015: Miguel Espinal (Yonkers, NY)

2015: Leroy Browning (Palmdale, CA)

2015: Kevin Matthews (Detroit, MI)

2015: Bettie Jones (Chicago, IL)

2015: Keith Childress Jr. (Las Vegas, NV)

2014: Akai Gurley (New York, NY)

2014: Tamir Rice (Cleveland, OH)

2014: Victor White III (Iberia Parish, LA)

2014: Dante Parker (San Bernardino County, CA)

2014: Ezell Ford (Los Angeles, CA)

2014: Michael Brown (Ferguson, MO)

2014: Tyree Woodson (Baltimore, MD)

2014: John Crawford III (Beavercreek, OH)

2014: Eric Garner (New York, NY)

2014: Yvette Smith (Bastrop, TX)

2014: Donitre Hamilton (Milwaukee, WI)

2014: Jordan Baker (Houston, TX)

2014: Rumain Brisbon (Phoenix, AZ)

2014: Kajieme Powell (St. Louis, MO)

2014: McKenzie Cochran (Southfield, MI)

2013: Andy Lopez (Santa Rosa, CA)

2013: Barrington Williams (New York, NY)

2013: Carlos Alcis (New York, NY)

2013: Deion Fludd (New York, NY)

2013: Jonathan Ferrell (Bradfield Farms, NC)

2013: Kimani Gray (New York, NY)

2013: Kyam Livingstone (New York, NY)

2013: Larry Eugene Jackson, Jr. (Austin, TX)

2013: Miriam Carey (Washington, DC)

2013: Tyrone West (Baltimore, MD)

2012: Chavis Carter (Jonesboro, AR)

2012: Dante Price (Dayton, OH)

2012: Duane Brown (New York, NY)

2012: Ervin Jefferson (Atlanta, GA)

2012: Jersey Green (Aurora, IL)

2012: Johnnnie Kamahi Warren (Dotham, AL)

2012: Justin Slipp (New Orleans, LA)

2012: Kendrec McDade (Pasadena, CA)

2012: Malissa Williams (Cleveland, OH)

2012: Nehemiah Dillard (Gainesville, FL)

2012: Ramarley Graham (New York, NY)

2012: Raymond Allen (Galveston, TX)

2012: Rekia Boyd (Chicago, IL)

2012: Reynaldo Cuevas (New York, NY)

2012: Robert Dumas, Jr. (Cleveland, OH)

2012: Sgt. Manuel Loggins, Jr. (Orange County, CA)

2012: Shantel Davis (New York, NY)

2012: Sharmel Edwards (Las Vegas, NV)

2012: Shereese Francis (New York, NY)

2012: Tamon Robinson (New York, NY)

2012: Timothy Russell (Cleveland, OH)

2012: Wendell Allen (New Orleans, LA)

2011: Alonzo Ashley (Denver, CO)

2011: Jimmell Cannon (Chicago, IL)

2011: Kenneth Chamberlain (White Plains, NY)

2011: Kenneth Harding (San Francisco, CA)

2011: Raheim Brown (Oakland, CA)

2011: Reginald Doucet (Los Angeles, CA)

2010: Aaron Campbell (Portland, OR)

2010: Aiyana Jones (Detroit, MI)

2010: Danroy Henry (Thornwood, NY)

2010: Derrick Jones (Oakland, CA)

2010: Steven Eugene Washington (Los Angeles, CA)

2009: Kiwane Carrington (Champaign, IL)

2009: Oscar Grant (Oakland, CA)

2009: Shem Walker (New York, NY)

2009: Victor Steen (Pensacola, FL)

2008: Tarika Wilson (Lima, OH)

2007: DeAunta Terrel Farrow (West Memphis, AR)

2006: Sean Bell (New York, NY)

2005: Henry Glover (New Orleans, LA)

2005: James Brisette (New Orleans, LA)

2005: Ronald Madison (New Orleans, LA)

2004: Timothy Stansbury (New York, NY)

2003: Alberta Spruill (New York, NY)

2003: Orlando Barlow (Las Vegas, NV)

2003: Ousmane Zongo (New York, NY)

2003: Michael Ellerbe (Uniontown, PA)

2001: Timothy Thomas (Cincinnati, OH)

2000: Earl Murray (Dellwood, MO)

2000: Malcolm Ferguson (New York, NY)

2000: Patrick Dorismond (New York, NY)

2000: Prince Jones (Fairfax County, VA)

2000: Ronald Beasley (Dellwood, MO)

1999: Amadou Diallo (New York, NY)

1994: Nicholas Heyward, Jr. (New York, NY)

1992: Malice Green (Detroit, MI)

1985: Edmund Perry (New York, NY)

1984: Eleanor Bumpurs (New York, NY)

1983: Michael Stewart (New York, NY)

1981: Ron Settles (Signal Hill, CA)

1979: Eula Love (Los Angeles, CA)

1969: Mark Clark (Chicago, IL)

1969: Fred Hampton (Chicago, IL)

1964: James Powell (New York, NY)

*Sandra Bland, who was found hanging in her jail cell in 2015, is not listed, as her death was officially ruled a suicide…though we know the truth.

11

All About that Bass <u>And</u> Treble

Truth Bomb:

#PlusSizePlease was started by Millennial blogger, Sarah Chiwaya, when she attended a fashion event and a garment she wanted wasn't available in her size. When she shared the image on social site Instagram, a follower asked if it was made in larger options. Chiwaya responded "no," followed by the soon-to-be popularized hashtag. Now, #PlusSize-Please is used across social media platforms to inspire brands to provide diverse sizing options of their garments.[1]

—

Body Image and Branding

Usually, the first thing I do when I wake up is observe myself in a full-length mirror that's situated by my bedside. I suck in my stomach, subject my arms to a jiggle test by waving, and turn 180 degrees to put my profile through some scrutiny, including debating if I see a double chin forming or noting the protrusion of my belly. After a couple of minutes, I snap out of my body image obsession, consciously repeating encouraging remarks such as those shared on social media outlets from body-advocacy group Healthy is the New Skinny. However, some self-doubt returns later as I go to get dressed and the thought of putting on jeans terrorizes me.

Though my body shape is common—larger thighs, smaller waist—finding a pair of affordable denim is challenging and prevents me from jean shopping at all. This is when I settle for a fit and flare skirt. For the rest of the day I continue to push myself to disregard self-disparaging remarks, even when coming across billboards with models showcasing an idealized body type or social media messaging with the same imaging.

Marketing has expanded to include not only traditional print, but also online advertising on social media sites. This makes escaping damaging body image messaging more difficult. Minute-to-minute use of social media channels like Instagram and Facebook includes newsfeeds dominated by body selfies of men and women partially clothed, fitness promotions of before and after shots that are normally staged, and models who characteristically feature a fair complexion and slender frame. Though these mass-market images have influence, Millennials are starting to wizen up and not rely on marketing to relay what beauty norms are. In fact, we increasingly challenge brands to normalize their campaigns. We want marketing campaigns to be less aspirational when it comes to beauty and image, and more reflective of us, the consumer.

After a few months working for a well-respected fashion brand, I realized that I was one of the very few employees not on a juice cleanse or strict diet, and this left me feeling insecure. It wasn't until I met plus-size model, Katie Wilcox, when heading to a photo studio one day that I started to change my perspective on body image. An alluring brunette with a twinkle in her eyes, she was confident, while possessing a certain cheekiness.

What was interesting about our encounter was that, when you saw her, she didn't live up to her categorization of plus-size. She was normal, her body type was normal, and, most importantly, she looked healthy. She joked that, in comparison to the models commonly hired, she did live up to the title. In response, I looked down to observe my own size-6 frame, and questioned if I, too, would be considered plus-sized. She then gave me an all-knowing smile that hinted she knew what I was thinking and asserted that there is a place for every body type to be positively recognized. Her mission was to make that space more visible and accessible to everyone.

Katie Wilcox, co-founder of Healthy is the New Skinny, is adamant on encouraging body-positive messaging, as well as pointing out negative marketing. When she comes across a glossy magazine cover or magazine spread that unconsciously feeds into our hateful body beliefs, she points it out on her social media channels with #NotBuyingIt. A *Shape* magazine editorial with the headline "Fast Track to Sexy" was one example she spotlighted. The spread featured a thin and fair-complexioned woman in a body-hugging mini dress power walking in heels, captioned, "Shrink every inch, while sculpting sleek muscle...".[2]

Wilcox heatedly responded, "In *Shape* Magazine they say the fast track to sexy is to shrink every inch!!! Well, I didn't realize that in order to be attractive I need to 'shrink' my entire body. This is straight-up garbage and we are #notbuyingit. Just another example of the messaging girls and women receive daily that leads them to believe their value is in sex, seeking approval from others, and being small. You are so much more than that!" After she posts, thousands of her readers re-post with their own enflamed remarks accompanied by actual body-positive sentiments.

In addition to calling out pejorative magazine advertising on social media, Millennials also confront specific brands head-on using the Web. Victoria's Secret is one of these brands that Gen-Yers will target for poor body-positive messaging. *The Perfect Body* campaign, for example, launched in 2014 featured the title of the campaign printed across extremely thin models. Frustrated 20-somethings posed in a viral image, flipping off this Victoria's Secret floor to ceiling storefront poster, and a Change.org petition created by two students, demanded that the lingerie-retailer reword their campaign. Though the brand cited "Body" was in reference to the type of bra, not a woman's shape, they adjusted their headline to read "A Body for Every Body."[3] Underwear brand Dear Kate also called out Victoria's Secret homogenous beauty and body standards by replicating the advertisement, this time featuring diverse models.[4]

Millennials work to reshape what people have been conditioned to view as normal when it comes to how we look. A few brands are starting to work with us in support of change, as well. When only 5% of women possess the ideal body type represented in mainstream media, Millennials have realized that brands seek to magnify our insecurities in order to sell us more products and services.

However, our involvement to address body image is now influencing how brands are doing their storytelling. As bestselling author and expert researcher Dan Schawbel notes on a consumer study he completed with Elite Daily, "Only 1% of Millennials surveyed said that a compelling advertisement would make them trust a brand more. Millennials believe that advertising is all spin and not authentic."[6] Thus, while clever marketing strategies are important, they are not significant enough to get Millennials to act. Instead, we are pushing brands to establish authenticity and social responsibility in order to attract and keep us as loyal customers.

While walking to lunch, I stopped to routinely admire poster advertising at a corner bus stop. Whether a new movie is being promoted, museum exhibit, or latest technology, I get a cultural fix just by examining what's current. This day, however, a particular ad made me smile. Lane Bryant's "I'm No Angel" poster, displaying six culturally- and body-diverse models in flirtatious and sexy underwear styles was empowering and a great response to Victoria's Secret campaigns that rely solely on similar-looking body types, heights, and even skin complexions for their models.[7] Immediately, I took photos and shared with friends, colleagues, and my online followers.

Body Image Insecurities

Body image in relation to weight has been a sensitive subject for me since early adolescence. Around the age of 12, my insecurities dominated, as is typical for anyone at this age. I became more aware of how different I was compared to peers, especially in regards to my under-developed body shape, something that made me stick out as a Black American living in a predominantly Black community. With a frame that only size double-zero clothing would cling to, teachers, social workers, and eventually my parents would begin to question if I had an eating disorder. Peers disarmed what little confidence I had by routinely confronting me about my waif-like frame and comparing it to their womanly, blossoming figures.

Despite the fact that I had a normal appetite, I started to engage in binge-eating, as well as overeating, to dispel rumors of anorexia and bulimia. This didn't help, however, as I was placed under surveillance in an outpatient facility, which initially started as a visit to help treat my depression. After ending treatment, however, I became increasingly paranoid and anxious, fearful that my parents and friends did not trust me. I now refused to go the restroom alone while in public and tried to ensure that someone was around if I had to use the bathroom at home. At that time in my life I was being thin-shamed, or made to feel insecure and invaluable as a result of my natural shape.

People who are overweight go through what's called fat-shaming, and the insecurity felt is very similar.

Influential author, speaker, and filmmaker Jean Kilbourne notes in *Killing Us Softly: Advertising's Image of Women* that young girls are often comfortable with their body image until they reach adolescence. Then they start to strive for the impossible beauty standards reflected in advertising.[8] For me, this meant striving for a figure with curves.

When I reached college, I was in a different cultural setting where Black American students made up less than 8% of the student body population. In this space, thin madness was the craze, and I ultimately felt conflicted. Throughout this time, my body started to mature, and now I was in a situation where I didn't want that to occur. I obsessively monitored my thigh gap, an unhealthy body-image trend, to ensure that I didn't gain too much weight and stand out. I would stand in front of a floor-length hallway mirror in my dorm, press my feet together, lock my knees, and examine how far apart my thighs were situated. I even gloated when a friend enviously exclaimed that I had a thigh gap, afterwards causing her to stand in front of the mirror and repeat my actions, though she walked away feeling defeated when her thighs touched. The psychological yo-yo of being the perfect size, whatever that entailed, took over once again.

By the time I graduated college, I went from being a size 0 to a size 4, and when I entered the working world, which involved joining the ranks at a well-known fashion brand, I had never felt more insecure. I wasn't alone. When I confided in a co-worker about my body-image insecurities, she revealed how she survived an eating disorder. She even shared with me before-and-after photos to lure me out of the trap of unhealthy thinking before I could progress to a state of inflicting physical damage.

I had stopped binge eating as I had done in high school, and now I was leaning toward deprivation. However, in that moment, I had made the choice to let it go. The National Eating Disorders Association shares that as of 2011, twenty million women and ten million men suffered from a clinically significant eating disorder at some time in their life, including anorexia nervosa, bulimia nervosa, binge-eating disorder, or an eating disorder not otherwise specified.[9]

Eating disorders are, unfortunately, still common, regardless of which generation a person identifies with. However, body image trends sparked by social media posts make it easier for youth to prescribe to and document. The thigh gap, for example, was one trend I latched on to in order to convince myself that, if I had it, I would be beautiful, but more modern trends include the belly-button challenge or Kylie Jenner lip challenge. Due to the rise of technology and social media, these trends are adapted as sport, encouraging women to photograph and tag themselves succeeding at accomplishing the trend or failing. The belly button challenge involves women placing their arm around their back in an attempt to reach their belly button from this position. If successful, they are hailed thin enough and, subsequently, healthy.[10]

The Kylie Jenner lip challenge, so named after the famous reality television star and model, encouraged women to mimic Jenner's full lips. What participants didn't realize was that Jenner had engaged in a lip plumping procedure done in a safe environment. Those who tried out the lip challenge attempted to recreate her look by sucking into the opening of a bottle for a dangerous amount of time, causing mouths to swell and bruise. The unexpected results were shared across social media networks, first out of humor and then as a cautionary tale. Eventually, the takedown of the lip challenge was swift, with protests ensuing.[11]

As a new breed of women surface, these social media challenges are likely to generate backlash faster. When Millennials like Katie Wilcox step in to police damaging trends, such as egging on other Gen-Yers to flip off the camera while trying the belly button challenge, we can create an online climate that calls out negative messaging for what it is. Similar to how my co-worker condemned my body-negativity, we can do the same for others.

Modern Millennial Celebrities Redefine Body Image

"Size zero-zero is the new zero," character Christina McKinney affirms after Betty astutely observes that the models being cast for a runway show are starting to appear thinner. On a typical Friday night—or any weekday—I'm enjoying *Ugly Betty*. Episode "Zero Worship" from season two is all about the fashion world's contribution to thin madness, asserting that being thin equates to being beautiful. Adolescents on the show are affected by the magazine's decision to feature emaciated models, and even throw away their lunchtime meals, assuming that, by doing so, they will be in vogue. When Betty comes face-to-face with youth who are plagued with thin-madness, by proxy of her nephew, she sets about to overturn their belief that in order to be beautiful you have to be skinny. By the end of the episode—spoiler alert—the runway show does not feature the unhealthily skeletal models who were initially cast, but a lineup of body-diverse women from all walks of life.[12]

Ugly Betty is a series set with a cast of characters working at elite fashion magazine *Mode* and, because of this setting, writers of the show can humorously explore touchy topics surrounding body image. Main character Betty is seen as the tipping point, swaying bad decisions to good. What makes her character so influential is that she's unaffected by the superfluous pressures of the fashion world and adopts the role of the moral compass, even affecting those who constantly mock her for her appearance, ethnicity, and weight. By the show relying on paradigms such as casting Betty's character as the "unlikely heroine," or supporting cast members as TV tropes "the self-absorbed blonde" or "well-to-do playboy," television can mirror specific truisms of our lives when it comes to issues like body image. As of late, this topic has become increasingly popular for Millennials, including Gen-Yers, who work in the entertainment industry.

Gen-Y actresses like Jennifer Lawrence and Mindy Kaling (yes, Mindy, you *can* sit with Millennials) for example, as well as model Cameron Russell are only a few out of many celebrities who are now using their platform to reinforce positive body-image messaging. Younger celebs are supremely conscious of how they are represented in the media, not skirting around topics of food and weight, as well as admitting being comfortable with and in their body. They are using their brand to create a culture where self-acceptance is key.

Lawrence has presented herself on numerous occasions as one who revels in the body positivity movement. She famously stated, "I would rather look chubby on screen and like a person in real life," to rebuff Hollywood's engineered body-exclusive standards. And her confessional-style antics show that she understands that her perfected look *is* the result of a team she pays for. Mindy Kaling, though technically a Gen-Xer (she missed the Millennial cut-off by a year, give or take) is another leading actress who's consistently outspoken about weight and body image. In a *Teen Vogue* profile, she stated, "I get so worried about girls with body image stuff… And I feel like I have been able to have a fun career and be an on-camera talent and be someone who has boyfriends and love interests and wears nice clothes and those kinds of things without having to be an emaciated stick. And it is possible to do it. In life, you don't have to be that way and you can have a great life, a fun life, and a fulfilling love life."[13]

One of my favorite role models for self-confidence and body acceptance, however, is model Cameron Russell. As part of the ubiquitous online audience, I constantly scour TED videos. I'm obsessed with self-help talks, psychology, and insights that enlighten what drives different facets of human behavior. One night, while sifting through potential videos to watch, I came across Russell's and, after watching, thought this adequately and intelligently reflects what I long to articulate when it comes to body image. For me Russell's talk featured life-changing statements that inspired what Oprah would regard an "ah-hah" moment.

Looks Aren't Everything; Believe Me, I'm a Model, has been viewed over 12 million times on TED.com alone, and superbly describes the very real dilemma little girls, adolescents, and women confront which I'll call the "if-only" syndrome. If only I were taller, if only I had longer hair, if only my nose looked different, etc. Essentially, if only I genetically possess the idealistic traits of beauty represented in media, then I will be happy.

Russell answers these theoretical posits by sophisticatedly stating, "…the thing that we [models] never say on camera, that I have never said on camera, is 'I am insecure'. And I'm insecure because I have to think about what I look like every day. And if you ever are wondering, 'If I have thinner thighs and shinier hair, will I be happier?' you just need to meet a group of models, because they have the thinnest thighs and the shiniest hair and the coolest clothes, and they're the most physically insecure women probably on the planet."

Another important point that I greatly appreciated in Russell's talk was her prescience on models being an object or product. She points out numerous images of her days before a modeling shoot, or days after, compared to an advertising campaign she's completed. "And I hope what you're seeing is that these pictures are not pictures of me. They are constructions, and they are constructions by a group of professionals, by hairstylists and makeup artists and photographers and stylists and all of their assistants and pre-production and post-production, and they build this. That's not me."[14] The before-and-after slideshow she presents hits on the fact that almost every image in advertising is digitally altered, thus no one, not even models, meets the absurd criteria of beauty imposed by the media.

As my body matured in my late teens and early 20s, I remember scouring the Internet, looking for celebrities I could identify with. In the age of the new millennium, where eating disorders were top tabloid stories, there was always a yo-yo of I want a healthy figure, but I also want to look like this up-and-coming starlet who may or may not have an eating disorder. I would Google names like Scarlett Johansson and Sandra Bullock who had a similar body shape as mine and suddenly feel confident. Now with modern-day Millennial celebrities, there is more openness surrounding body-diversity and adolescents don't have to search to find a role model. In that way, Gen-Yers are inducing an inclusive culture that's healthier inside and out.

Popular Body-Positive Campaigns

Every time I see a new body-diverse advertising campaign, as a consumer, I am quick to promote it as well as share my gratification on social media. In fact, most of my friends are, and this is because Millennials rely heavily on user-generated reviews to make or break a brand. This is important, as Western culture's obsession with the female body and controlling its representation in the media has reached horrific levels from both the media and audiences. Now Millennials can vocalize frustrations and police pejorative advertising, while subsequently rewarding businesses that are doing the right thing, all through social media. This gives way to more brands adopting socially responsible messaging and practices, as they know Gen-Yers are holding them accountable. Dove, Special K, and even BuzzFeed are a few well-known businesses that have made efforts to renew public interest, both in the online world and in real life, to help women feel confident and body positive.

The Dove Campaign for Real Beauty, launched in 2004, was a multi-phase project that continued through 2007. It was pegged a social mission to educate and influence all women, eliminating biases of race, culture, nationality, and age, as well as genetic factors such as body shape or looks. The tagline for this campaign provoked women to "Imagine a World Where Beauty is a Source of Confidence, Not Anxiety," encouraging women and Millennials to discuss things like beauty issues or the role of media relegating body image standards.

Dishearteningly, through Dove's study, they found that, globally, only 2% of women describe themselves as beautiful, signaling that beauty, body image and self-worth are, in some ways, interdependent. By exploring, and ultimately unpacking, beauty stereotypes engrained by media practices, Dove has used its own power as an entity to start to reshape negative body-image ideals.

One of my favorite body-positive projects from Dove aired in September of 2006 when the brand released, *Evolution*, a 60-second video, as a latter part of their campaign. The short film deconstructed beauty ideology in time-lapse fashion, by taking an everyday woman and transforming her into a model.

The emphasis was on the process of alteration and how the progression of changing one's image to conform is a construct. This was all in an effort to demonstrate that what women aspire to look like can be unnatural and, in most cases, unattainable. Female consumers have been encouraged to emulate characteristics that only 5% of the population has, as well as achieve the looks of models who have been digitally altered with image manipulation software like PhotoShop. To reverse what the media sells us, which is the need to be "beautiful" in order to be valued, the goal is to empower women to define beauty for themselves. This is what Dove accomplishes with this video.[15]

Special K, under the Kellogg umbrella, is another brand making attempts to carve out body-confident messaging. In 2012, they featured a plus-size model in one of their British campaigns, and previous to that, in 2011, the "What will you gain when you lose?" promotion began. The divisive brand advertising surfaced throughout various print, television, and online media advertisements, making an effort to laud women for being conscious about their health, while simultaneously not confusing healthiness with thinness. Their marketing campaign took women and put them into what can be a body-shaming situation, where they were prompted to step on a larger-than-life scale. Instead of receiving a number, an inspirational message appeared. The reactions of the women were videoed and shared. Though the marketing effort tried to reverse negative messaging, the campaign was lost on some, even prompting a Change.org petition.

In 2013 they launched another promotion "More Than a Number," this time centering on a pop-up shop where women shopping for denim were presented with an encouraging message instead of a numerical size. As I mentioned earlier, I experience my own paralysis when putting on jeans, coupled with a wave of insecure thoughts. This is something I go through daily, especially when I pull denim from freshly completed laundry and I have to do lunges to squeeze into them.

When the video from their campaign appeared, I realized that what felt like a solitary experience of self-doubt was a collective one and something that most women go through. Opening remarks from "More Than a Number" featured snippets from women vocalizing their dislikes and insecurities. The first audio clip starts with "I hate shopping for jeans...," followed by the voice of another woman who says, "It's always so painful..." After a series of dispirited comments, the text "Why do we let the size of our jeans measure our worth?" materializes. Next, we see women entering the pop-up shop by Special K, scanning through racks of denim. As they spot a pair of jeans that they like, they go to check the size and realize that the jeans they want don't have numerical measurements but a positive adjective, like "radiant." The message "You are so much more than a number," appears as the closing statement.[16]

Internet news site BuzzFeed is an online space that loves to update newsfeeds with content that, in some ways, reflects how inclusive Gen-Y is becoming. I frequently visit BuzzFeed for their niche listicles and videos as a resource for breaking news, statistics, and follow-up opinions on major events, both domestically and internationally. I also check out their site to feel in sync with other Millennials. Their insightful video, titled *What Do Strangers Think of You?* is one of my favorite pieces they've shared and underlines how the characteristics we want to change when we look in the mirror may be what a stranger finds the most beautiful.

The short experiment records both Millennial men and women pointing out their insecurities, as they unknowingly stand in front of a two-way mirror. People on the other side share their first thoughts about the person they are observing and they, too, are unaware that who they are describing are in the process of vocalizing frustrations they have with their body. For example, on one side of the mirror, a man describes how much he hates his cheekbones, while, on the other side, those surveying him say they are immediately attracted to his cheekbones. The experiment illustrates how we've been trained to view features about ourselves as unattractive, because, unconsciously, we favor the streamlined traits presented to us every day in the media.[17]

The intention of these experiments is to start to reverse the damaging effects of everyday advertising. As the nature of marketing relies on generating an emotional response to trigger a reaction from consumers, our insecurities are slated to become the driving factor for instigating a sale. However, the popularity of the promotions from Dove, Special K, and BuzzFeed show that there is support in changing up advertisements. Taking cues from Millennials, brands can adapt to the needs of today's consumer, extending the reach of the product or service, while remaining relevant to the customer.

Groundbreaking Body Image Movements in Waking Life

Ninety-one percent of women are unhappy with their bodies, and resort to diet and exercise with the intention of altering their body shape.[18] There is no secret that advertising sells us concepts of normality: they teach us what is beautiful, what is standard, and, with some regard, what our value systems should be. Every calculated marketing formula always comes back to money. How much money can businesses in the fashion and beauty industries make utilizing our insecurities as capital?

Millennials are buying into this less, and as brands recognize the shift in consumer behavior, groundbreaking body image movements occur. From using plus-size models more or models of different ethnicities and disabled models, we are changing what defines body image norms.

Mentioned earlier, in 2012, Special K started favoring plus size, or real women, in an effort to teach that weight loss should be linked to health. A representative stated, "It is the perfect way to encourage women not just to focus on the bathroom scales." Other brands, including Calvin Klein, have indirectly encouraged body-shape diversity, as well.

Size-10 model, Myla Dalbesio, booked a spot for their 2014 lingerie ad, along with other industry-standard-sized models, for example. Though the brand never heralded the phrase "plus-size" to describe Dalbesio, social media threw around the term when noting that the campaign featured a normal size-10 woman. Myla Dalbesio spoke about this on *The Today Show,* stating, "I think that Calvin Klein has done something that's really groundbreaking, which is they released this campaign with what some would say is a normal-size model, a size 10. And size-10 girls, there's not a lot of spots for us to fit in the fashion industry."[19]

Tess Holliday, born Tess Munster, is another plus-size model and body-love activist who was the first size-22 model to sign with MiLK Model Management and the largest plus-size model to be booked by a traditional modeling agency. Her social media campaign #effyourbeautystandards started on Instagram in 2013 and, as she explains to *The Huffington Post,* "I created the hashtag because I was tired of being told what I could and couldn't wear by the media and how I should cover my body because of my size."[20]

Other landmark moments in fashion include those from models Jillian Mercado, Dr. Danielle Sheypuk, and Karen Crespo, women who have been featured either in print or on runway, eschewing socializations of what a typical model should look like.

Fashion blogger and model, Mercado, for example, battles muscular dystrophy. However, this did not stop Diesel artistic director, Nicola Formichetti, from putting her in a print advertisement that would later be featured in *Vogue* and *Interview*. For the campaign named "reboot," Mercado coolly posed in a wheelchair, her platinum coiffure, worker man's denim shirtdress, and bright red lips showcasing her strength as a public fashion figure who's both beautiful and ballsy. Mercado, earning her veteran status in the fashion industry, shared with the *Daily Beast*, "I knew I was throwing myself into the fire when I wanted to work in fashion… I work equally as hard as everyone else does in this industry, and my chair doesn't give me permission to slack off," she says. "My passion is equal to yours—I just come with a chair that moves."[21]

Designer Carrie Hammer has been another crucial figure and role model for inhibiting body diversity using the runway to welcome disabled models such as Dr. Danielle Sheypuk and Karen Crespo in her New York Fashion Week shows. In an email interview with the website Women's eNews, Hammer says, "I made the decision to cast role models, not runway models. It is so important to me that women have positive body image and are empowered in work and their life. My line makes dresses to fit women. We don't make dresses that women need to fit into."[22]

Because of Carrie Hammer's vigor for diverse body representation and overall stereotype defying mentality, Dr. Danielle Sheypuk and Karen Crespo, as well as other headlining models for 2014, were able to oppose mainstream beauty and body image conventions. Sheypuk became the first person to own a spot on a fashion runway in a wheelchair, successfully chipping away at closeted image ideals, while Crespo, a quadruple amputee, was also able to make her runway debut at Hammer's Fashion Institute show at NY Fashion Week.

Runways are only one avenue where the masses are encouraged to interact with inclusive body types and beauty standards. In the everyday world, however, one woman is making an effort to uphold non-traditional beauty beliefs as well. Australian journalist Tracey Spicer ensnared over one million viewers with her TEDxSouthBank-Women talk, owning up to the fact that she is a "vain fool." During her talk *The Lady Stripped Bare,* she shares her antipathy for standardized beauty ideas, revealing the fact that women, on average, spend 27 minutes in the morning to get ready, equating to 10 full working days over a span of a year.

To complement her candid speech, she removed her makeup on stage, revealing a fresh-faced TV personality. But her Ted Talk was not the only step forward she would take. She also made news for vowing to go without makeup for a full year, though, at the conclusion of that span of time, she shared her certainty to never revisit grueling beauty routines. She relishes in the process of learning how to strip away more as she makes way for the "new norm."[23]

Major transitions are happening, ranging from celebrity culture to mass-market advertising. Commercialized beauty isn't blotted out entirely, yet positive changes are impactful and occurring more frequently. Even the imperial "heroine-chic" days have faded into obsolescence as we welcome bodies of all shapes and sizes. By encouraging women and men to define their own standards of beauty, Millennials are empowering ourselves and others to be body-positive, body-inclusive, and body-strong.

Fifteen Body-Positive Anthems

1) "Baby Got Back" by Sir Mix A Lot

2) "My Humps" by The Black Eyed Peas

3) "Bootylicious" by Destiny's Child

4) "Video" by India Arie

5) "Beautiful" by Christina Aguilera

6) "I'm Too Sexy" by Right Said Fred

7) "F**kin' Perfect" by P!nk

8) "Firework" by Katy Perry

9) "I am the Body Beautiful" by Salt-n-Pepa

10) "Hard out Here" by Lily Allen

11) "Put Your Records On" by Corinne Bailey Rae

12) "Konichiwa Bitches" by Robyn

13) "Unpretty" by TLC

14) "Work That" by Mary J. Blige

15) "All About that Bass" by Meghan Trainor

12

Self(ie)-Obsessed

Truth Bomb:

At the 2014 Google developer's conference, then Senior Vice President—and now CEO of Google Inc.—Sundar Pichai revealed that 93 million selfies are taken every day using devices running on Android.[1]

—

History of the Selfie

Chin out, eyes narrowed in the style of Peter Hurley's masterful tutorial "It's All About the Squinch!"—smizing (smiling with your eyes), phrasing creatively coined by supermodel Tyra Banks, also applicable. If desiring to show teeth, press your tongue against the back of your pearly whites to avoid over grinning. After finding your light (another modeling tip from Banks), hold camera steady and start photographing. Finally, employ a filter to enhance the original photo, but only if needed.

These are the best practices that go with selfie-taking, and each one floods my thoughts in a matter of seconds when posing for a photo. The above suggestions, picked up from television shows, online posts, and fashion magazines, cater to the desire to look attractive and instantly share pictures online by way of social media. However, this mania isn't exclusive to me, as selfies are ingrained in our everyday culture.

I can trace the start of selfie-taking fanaticism back to the Myspace era. Angst-burdened peers would post dark, black and white photos, while those who were popular attempted to mimic ideas of sexiness prevalent in popular culture. Though the word 'selfie' was beginning to emerge in conversations (it started to appear in discussions more when photographer Jim Krause used it in 2005)[2], the act had already invaded the online sphere. When the trend of taking selfies didn't die down, I conceded in taking a few of my own with a Kodak digital camera as my device of choice.

Climbing on top of the counter in my bathroom and facing a wall-to-wall mirror, I would stand with hips squared and the top of my body folded over. I had captured what I had considered to be a seductive pose, the kind I had seen in *Teen Vogue*. The distracting flash-decal would always be present in the photo, washing out my hand with a flare of light. Afterward, I would position the camera upward while holding my chin down with a smirk, characterizing the look of someone knowing something they shouldn't. This had been my foray into selfie-taking and, at the time, I considered myself an "artist." A decade later, I would spend hours trying to remember the login to my Myspace account to delete the embarrassing photos.

When it comes to selfie types, Millennials always find creative ways to make any occasion a camera-ready moment. Selfie styles that we capture regularly, and that have evolved from the mirror shot, include gym selfies, boob selfies, brelfies (breast-feeding selfies), bathroom selfies, ab selfies, and photo-with-a-celebrity selfies. We can also capture action-packed selfies, whether that means scaling a high-rise or snapping a photo surfing in the barrel of a wave, with help from the ingenious GoPro camera.

The selfie, in all of its variations, is icono-graphic of Millennial culture. The act of taking a selfie has been glamorized in club anthems including the song "#SELFIE" by The Chainsmokers, celebrated by pop stars like Katy Perry who will invite an audience member onstage with her to snap a photo, and crooned about by entertainers— Mindy Kaling's chapter dedicated to her own selfies in the hilarious book *Is Everyone Hanging Out Without Me? (And*

Other Concerns), being both comical and ingenuous. The song "Flawless," from hit maker and iconic singer Beyoncé, inspired a new option—the bed selfie—that other celebrities and the general population quickly adopted. Witnessing how pervasive selfie-taking is in today's culture, where did it actually begin?

We know that Myspace helped make selfie-taking popular via social connectivity, but the start of selfies interestingly dates back to 1839. Robert Cornelius, a photographer and chemist, produced a daguerreotype of himself, which became the first documented photo of this type.[3]

In the 1900s, Kodak's Brownie Box camera made the self-portraiture technique a bit easier, but it wasn't until the arrival of point-and-shoot cameras, and later mobile phone cameras, that made selfie-taking mainstream.[4] Now, technological advance-ments, including Apple iPhone's evolved front-facing camera that initially hit markets in 2010, and the addition of the ingenious front flash added to the camera in 2015, simplified taking a high-quality photo. In this way, taking a selfie is no longer about the painstaking process, but the story you can tell about yourself with an image.

By college, I had stopped using MySpace, parting ways with my awkward early teenage years and first selfies. I switched over to Facebook and I needed new photos, especially one to occupy the slot of the glorious profile picture. Fortunately, my first week at university allowed for the opportune moment to get the perfect selfie.

Arms outstretched, I marched with a brigade of other students from my residence hall. My dorm had initiated a zombie attack on our neighbors. The other dorm prepared water balloons, squirt guns, and hoses in a standoff. The attack lasted for almost an hour, and when the night had ended, groups of us posed together to take a zombie selfie. This became one of the first selfies I took in college and one of the first ones I shared on Facebook.

Using Selfies to Sell and Tell Stories

Selfies position Millennials as content creators, and companies are learning how to incorporate Gen-Yers' selfie-taking into marketing techniques. According to the *Business Insider* article "Selfies and Smartphone Video Are Changing Marketing," expertly written by Ira Kalb, selfies are used for promotion, branding, and distribution strategies.

Kalb writes, "Brand marketers are hunting for selfies and hauling videos that show their brands in a positive light, advertisers are incorporating them into their ads to communicate positive benefits of their products, and market researchers are using them to research how their products are being used in the marketplace."[5] One company does this perfectly.

GoPro, creatively dubbed as the most versatile camera in the world, enables exciting, shareable content that is person-centric by encouraging action-inspired selfies. In this way, consumers get to tell their story through selfies, which, in turn, promotes the GoPro narrative. Expert content marketing manager Kara Burney points this out, writing, "GoPro gamifies the submission of user-generated content through their Photo of the Day and Video of the Day contests. In fact, nine out of the top ten most-engaged-with photos from GoPro's Instagram account in 2014 were winners of the Photo of the Day Contest."[6]

Brands like AXE men's deodorant and BaubleBar jewelry have also used consumer-led initiatives like selfies. AXE previously hosted selfie challenges, including the multi-layered #KissForPeace campaign. The tactic to use selfies helped promote International Peace Day, a day of non-violence and ceasefire around the globe. The campaign featured multiple videos including a 60-second and shorter 30-second commercial, "Love," which aired during Super Bowl XLVIII and was again promoted on Valentine's Day. The initiative encouraged couples to pucker up and take a selfie, tagging the photo with the KissForPeace hashtag.

This selfie campaign continued up until International Day of Peace, September 21st.[7]

BaubleBar jewelry also utilized selfie-taking to boost community involvement and make the process of shopping online feel less brand-centric and more personalized. The company accomplished this by encouraging shoppers to take a selfie with the jewelry they purchased, upload to social media, and demarcate with #BaubleBar. In the past, Baublebar would even share pictures of fans in their jewelry on a portal for user-generated content called "The Download."

Examining what helps make selfies an accessible social media marketing tool that brands can easily take advantage of, we can look at mobile apps. Prior to photo apps, selfie-taking was a clunky process. Uploading an image from a point-and-shoot camera, saving it to a computer, attempting to edit the image, and uploading multiple photos to an album on Facebook, one of the few social media tools available in addition to Myspace, could take hours. Now we are able to capture a high-quality image immediately, as well as crop, edit, and manipulate our photos on our device, within minutes. Additionally, we are not limited to the platforms where we can share our images. Powerful picture-taking and video-streaming apps Instagram and Snapchat, in addition to Facebook, are popular outlets available at the push of a button.

To demonstrate the influence of these apps, we can look at numbers that detail user engagement. Sprout Social, a social media management tool, effectively notes that the picture-sharing app Instagram "...delivered brands 58 times more engagement per follower than Facebook and 120 times more engagement per follower than Twitter."[8]

Mobile app Snapchat is also impressive when it comes to user engagement. Digital storyteller and social media marketer Kate Talbot notes, "With over 100 million daily active users and 400 million snaps per day, Snapchat is one of the fastest-growing social networks. As you might already assume, 71% of Snapchat's U.S. users fall into the 18 to 34 age range. Even if your audience doesn't fall in that demographic, Snapchat is becoming a vital part of global marketing strategies."[9] As these mobile apps continue to flourish, so does selfie taking, enabling us to both sell and tell our stories.

Since the day I took my first selfie with my Kodak digital camera, I have amassed thousands of images, including those embarrassing mirror shots. I have memorable ones from college, and selfies that have demarcated celebratory life events, like me at a new job. Unlike the ingenuity of reality television stars Kim Kardashian and Kylie Jenner, however, I have yet to use my selfies to build a successful fan-base across social media profiles. I have, though, used the selfie to continue to tell my story and share a bond across the many generations in my family. Here's one particular memory that I will never forget...

Traveling from California to Georgia, my mom and I said goodbye to our warm weather for a week and headed to the surprisingly cold and rainy south. We were going to visit my grandmother in her assisted living home. Of course, our travels prompted airplane selfies, as well as photos waiting in the terminal while we trekked across country.

When we arrived, my grandmother barely recognized my mom and me, even after we lovingly pointed out the photos of ourselves on her bedroom wall. Her Alzheimer's was worsening. For a moment, though, a spark of knowing flashed in her eyes and we were hopeful—if only in that split second—that she would remember us.

To celebrate one of the last moments with all of us together, we huddled close and took multiple selfies, my grandmother posing as coolly as a person accustomed to being in front of the camera. The act didn't elude her. Naturally, she shared her confident side, smirking as the flash went off. She wasn't ready for her close up; she was ready for her selfie.

Five Famous Selfie Trends You May (or May Not) Have Forgotten About

1) Duckface—Lips pursed together in an exaggerated pout, sometimes combined with come-hither eyes, the duckface was one of the most popular selfie poses of 2013. Aiming to capture an expression that was sexy and evocative of a supermodel, the over-pouted look ended up resembling a duck. The trend has since faded, inspiring parodies, like babies duck-facing, on its way out.

2) Driving Selfies—In 2013, driving selfies prompted people to snap a shot or short video of him or herself behind the wheel of a car, boat, or even airplane. In a November 2013 article, CNN reported that there were "more than 3,727 posts under the #drivingselfie hashtag, more than 1,869 for the plural #drivingselfies, and more than 9,700 for #drivingtowork."[10] The trend hasn't completely gone away, however more and more people are proactively pledging to steer clear of distracted driving.

3) Bear Selfies—Bear selfies dominated in 2014, where adventure-stricken youth were ready to capture a self-portrait with a bear in the background. Lake

Tahoe was one destination where too many visitors were cited taking a bear selfie, even darting across highways to snap a photo with a bear.

In an interview with digital media site, Mashable, public affairs officer Lisa Herron reaffirmed, "We just want to remind people to stay on the trails and respect the wildlife. If you encounter a bear, it's best to back away slowly to another area." The U.S. Forest service additionally advised visitors against the harebrained action, stating the obvious: bears are unpredictable and can inflict harm.[11]

4) Pretty Girls Making Ugly Faces—Another 2014 trend, this selfie was popularized by the fun and quirky #PrettyGirlsMakingUglyFaces subreddit and tumblr, two popular social sharing sites. The gist of this selfie fad involved a before and after shot of a woman, one where she posed attractively and another where she intentionally produced an ugly expression. She would create the unflattering look by flaring her nostrils, double chinning herself, and crossing her eyes.

5) Faux Surprise Face—Writer Andrea Romano humorously cited the Faux Surprise Face as Duck Face 2.0 in early January of 2015. The Faux Surprise Face sounds exactly like what it is: Eyes wide, lips parted in a jaw-dropped fashion, and eyebrows

lifted to depict an expression of shock or amazement.[12]

13

Waiting for My Owl

Truth Bomb:

Rowling shared in an Amazon UK interview that when thinking of the names for the four Hogwart's houses, she wrote them down on the back of "an aeroplane sick bag." To our relief, the bag was empty.[1]

—

Though years have passed and I am a long way away from that fifth-grade classroom where my teacher established a routine of reading a chapter from *Harry Potter and The Sorcerer's Stone* daily, I am still patiently waiting for my Hogwarts acceptance letter. Did my owl get lost?

Harry Potter, a mega-machine of fantasy, has kept Millennials enchanted for most of our developing lives. My first introduction with this moving tale of camaraderie, heroism, struggle, and magic occurred when I was ten years old, and would evolve into a lifelong friendship. My fifth-grade teacher kicked off this bond not only with me, but with other students in my class as well. Reading one chapter day after day to perky-eared students who couldn't wait for more, we all welcomed the story of *Harry Potter and The Sorcerer's Stone*, eager for the end of lessons so Ms. Rose could pick up where we had left off the afternoon before.

Harry Potter has been more than a literary read: the story is an escape, one that lures readers into finishing hundreds of pages in days. The success of the series is reflective of our infallible desire to follow and vicariously experience the hero's journey. Similar to Tolkien's *The Lord of the Rings* trilogy, or even the episodic *Star Wars*, Rowling assigns a lot of power to a seemingly ordinary character who readers envision emulating, especially young readers. And it just so happened that for Millennials, this world of light and dark blossomed at a time when the majority of us were the same age as the protagonist, making for an alliance that would only strengthen as both reader and character matured.

At the beginning of the series, we are introduced to Harry Potter, who is 11 years old. Locked in a closet under a staircase, a space that serves as his bedroom, he lives with his cruel aunt, uncle, and cousin who adopted him after the death of his parents. They emphatically make him aware that he is the outcast in the family. Harry Potter, as readers later discover, is famous in a parallel wizarding world, but at the beginning of the first book he is not aware of his back-story, celebrity, or influence.

Because of this introduction, Rowling effortlessly creates a connection between the protagonist and reader, using his turbulent home life as a way to build empathy. When Harry Potter hit American markets, families experienced tough emotional fallouts due to divorce that left many single-parent homes. As a result, children caught in the middle of their parents' separation faced distress.

The idea of the *Leave it to Beaver* household increasingly diminished for Millennials, with parents and even grandparents splitting from their partners. This left a lot of us in states of guilt, confusion, anxiety, and depression. Coupled with part of the Millennial generation transitioning to teenagers, we often came to the conclusion that we were in this turbulence alone, fervently hoping that someone out there could possibly understand us. The *Harry Potter* series was that escape.

It was the summer the fifth book in the series, *Harry Potter and the Order of the Phoenix,* was released. I was 12, on the cusp of turning 13, and I craved the camaraderie of the popular trio, Harry, Hermione, and Ron, adopting them as my own friends when I read each page and peered into their adventures. Every book after the first had only taken me days to finish. I ravenously consumed word after word, page after page, chapter after chapter of this distant, but, in some cases, all too familiar world where the underdog was attempting to navigate adolescence.

Middle school was beginning soon, and the only thing I believed was that no one, including students, teachers, or my parents, understood me. I was labeled the awkward other who loved to read, who was charismatic about studying, and outside of school life had to face an unstable household. Harry Potter, although fictional, *did* understand what I was going through. We bonded over our battle scars of trauma, personal loss, and even abuse, as his vitriolic relationship with his guardians, the Dursley's, mirrored the violent one that I had with my dad. Even if no one else was there, Harry was, and that thought alone was enough to keep me going through my early teen years.

As Millennial readers matured with Harry and his friends, Hermione and Ron, we realized that these characters were up against the same challenges we experienced. We aged with this magical story, going through similar emotional growing pains, struggles with our "otherness" and search for identity, all while maneuvering coursework and whatever home life awaited us after school hours were over. Millennials longed for the adventures Harry and his two companions had in order to feel that we weren't alone, and they helped us cope when, in our own lives, there was little room for light, and darkness seemed to prevail. Harry Potter was that bright spot we needed to make it out of that darkness.

J.K. Rowling acknowledges through the Harry Potter series that tough life events and transitions are out of our control, but they don't have to change us for the worse. Thus, the universal feeling of being alone and going through something alone softens when we pick up any of the Harry Potter books.

An article posted on BuzzFeed confirmed this when multiple people remarked that the *Harry Potter* series saved them during difficult episodes in their life ranging from someone going through treatment for cancer or another struggling with mental health and contemplating suicide.[2] The story instilled that we *could* end up the hero of our story no matter what, and, in that way, Harry Potter affirmed that not only were our experiences valid, but so were we.

For many, the allure of Harry Potter comes from the idea of the hero's journey and our quest as readers to identify with the everyday person who is capable of so much more than meets the eye. But what makes the narrative even stronger and more dynamic is Rowling's capacity to represent both men and women as heroes, reaching an even wider fan base.

The development of Hermione Granger's character, for example, is one where she's made to be assertive, diminishing status quo "feminine" or "girly" traits that could have framed her as an overly sexualized supporting character or under-sexualized companion, only taken seriously due to a lack of physical attraction. Instead, Rowling created her as intelligent, emotionally stalwart, and driven, all while being a character who was neither cherished for her looks nor discredited for them. Hermione's sharp intellect made her an exemplary student, something I could relate to, and, though her brainy disposition sometimes left her as an outcast, her smarts helped save the lives of Harry and Ron not just once, but throughout the entirety of the book series.

Other powerful women in Rowling's series include Molly and Ginny Weasley, Professor Minerva McGonagall, and Luna Lovegood. Though there were several plot threads that followed some of these characters' love interests, they did not eclipse or downplay women as lovelorn supporting characters incapable of making impactful decisions. Instead, women and men both contribute to the betterment of the storyline, women being equally heroic, and, in the case of Bellatrix Lestrange, villainous.

After my nighttime class, I ran to my car, Hermione costume intact, and headed downtown to the local theatre. I was in college now, but remained a loyal fan of the Harry Potter series, bound to the books that had gotten me out of so many dark moments. My friends had already been camped out for the better part of the morning, afternoon, and now evening, along with hundreds of other moviegoers, waiting for the midnight release of *Harry Potter and The Deathly Hallows Part I.* This would be the last time my college friends and I would camp out together, as we were all graduating before the release of the final film.

I parked several blocks away under the starry-skied evening and hiked to the theatre, cradling my wand, memorizing spells, and perfecting my English accent. Typically, this would have been strange, but magic was in the air, sibilant and seemingly omnipresent. Lines of people snaked around dark corners and through alleyways, interrupting crosswalks; everywhere, would-be strangers united by the spellbound artistry Rowling had created with her book series.

I floated through the tail end of the line, making my way to the middle of the crowd as if I were on the back of a thrashing basilisk, until I reached my friends. Lightning scars decorated foreheads and the dark mark intruded on forearms of others. There I joined the group, two bobby pins clasping back part of my naturally frizzy hair, wand and spells ready, and confident, a word that I was just learning to attribute to myself, thanks to Hermione

Granger and Rowling. This was a little piece of our childhood that my friends and I got to share together that night under the stars.

In her stories, Rowling made both men and women equally significant to drive the plot forward, covered topics on family dissonance, death, bullying, and stigma, and even later revealed that one of the lead characters, Headmaster Dumbledore, was homosexual.[3] Because of this, she has attracted fans from all walks of life. Her prowess at dancing with all of these powerful themes and intertwining them in such a palatable fashion made this book series a mega-success that still matriculates through generations.

Her series is so ingrained in cultures all over the world today, that over 400 million copies of the *Harry Potter* book series have sold, and globally the movies have banked over $7 billion, excluding DVD sales, which brought in almost $2 billion additionally in revenue.

Harry Potter has also been translated into an estimated 69 languages cementing themes of heroism and love as universal.[4] Correlating with the success of the books and movies, costumes, paraphernalia, Jellybeans, Starbucks secret recipes, beer flavors, tribute theme parks, spinoff stories, and loads of other goodies inspired by the Harry Potter empire have left many of us muggles continuously enthralled by this beautiful, still-thriving, fantastical realm created by author J.K. Rowling, even after the books and films have ended.

The story of Harry Potter coming to life during the school age of Generation-Y in 1997 and ending nearly a decade and a half later, with the final movie released in 2011, is why this series has become the book and movie of Millennials. Though Harry Potter began to attract all generations, the story prospered in unison with the maturation of Gen-Yers. An unbreakable reader-character connection stemmed from Millennials being able to witness the experiences of Harry Potter and live through the same tragedies and subsequent victories echoed in our everyday lives, from personal loss to family discord. His defeats were ours, and ours seemingly felt like his. And while we Millennials may not have a snow-colored carrier owl delivering an acceptance letter to Hogwarts School of Witchcraft and Wizardry, we get to enjoy something even more magical: a lifetime of friendship and adventure.

Seven Magical Facts for Fancying and Forgetful Muggles

Though there are quite a number of Harry Potter fans, for some the magical trio of Harry, Ron, and Hermione remains a mystery. The following are seven magical facts, as well as tidbits, about the series to either pique your interest or further your knowledge on the wonderful world of Harry Potter:

1) J.K. Rowling vulnerably shares in an interview that the passing of her mother six months into the writing of Harry Potter was the reason she kept going with the series. Rowling's mother did not know she had started writing the series. Rowling states, "If she hadn't died, I don't think it's too strong to say that there wouldn't be *Harry Potter*. The books are what they are because she died...because I loved her and she died."[5]

2) Dementors, or "soulless creatures," that siphon all sensations of happiness, joy, love, and intelligence by way of a kiss or an indrawn breath, are a physical representation of Rowling's experience with depression. Dementors are faceless beings cloaked in black robes, and whenever they are near, all

happiness seems to drain from the world as they create an icy, pitch-black landscape filled with emptiness and sorrow.[6]

3) Contrary to popular belief, the 't' at the end of Voldemort is silent, as his name is French and means "flight of death."[7]

4) The idea for Sirius Black's tattoos came from those used in Russian prison gangs. The markings identify the person as someone to be feared and respected.[8]

5) In the film *Harry Potter and the Deathly Hallows Part II*, when it is revealed that Harry isn't dead, George turns to share this moment with his twin, but then realizes there's no one there.

6) Natalie McDonald, who appears on page 159 of *Harry Potter and The Goblet of Fire*, was a real person. She was a nine-year-old girl from Toronto, Canada, who was dying of leukemia. She wrote to J.K. Rowling, asking what was going to happen in the next Harry Potter book, as she would not live long enough to read it. The author emailed back, but Natalie had died a day earlier. In tribute, she became a first-year student at Hogwarts placed by the Sorting Hat in Gryffindor—the house for the brave at heart—in the fourth book.[9]

7) Once, in an online chat with fans, J.K. Rowling revealed that the third scent Hermione could smell emanating from the Amortentia (love potion) was that of Ron Weasley's hair.[10]

14

Can You Repeat That?
(Millennial Slang)

Now that you've made it through to the end, here are some definitions of the most popular words Millennials use in day-to-day conversations, whether discourse happens in person, online, or via text messages, to keep you informed.

1) Catfish–Inspired by the 2010 documentary of the same name,[1] catfish means to be duped or hoodwinked when it comes to online dating. A person will hide their true identity, using a fake persona on social media or dating profiles. Ex. Girl or guy meets girl or guy online. A relationship unfolds and although one party may want to meet in person, the other is reluctant. This can go on for months or even a year, until it is discovered that the reluctant party is a completely different person than

who they said they were online. The victim has been "catfished."

2) Ghosting–When communication abruptly ends between two people who are dating (i.e. A girl or guy stops texting, calling, or interacting online by way of social media with someone with whom they were romantically involved). This happens unexpectedly or out of the blue. The victim of ghosting might continue to reach out, unaware of what occurred to trigger radio silence, but will oftentimes never receive a response again.

3) FOMO–Stands for "Fear of Missing Out" and refers to the dread that one event, party, or social gathering may be cooler than the one a person chooses to attend. This creates an anxiety that this person is left out of experiencing something better.

4) Bae–A term of endearment and affection. Syn. Babe.

5) Bronies–Teenage or young adult male viewers who enjoy the television show *My Little Pony*.

6) Bro–Typically an obnoxious college-aged male who loves to party. Bros are often, though not exclusively, fraternity members. Bros will be photographed holding red cups and sporting polos.[2]

7) Lumbersexual–A male who revels in the retro-lumberjack style. This may include, but is not limited

to, a metrosexual man sporting a finely trimmed but burly beard, along with a flannel, plaid-patterned shirt.

8) Hipster–Signifies a subculture of middle- and upper-class 20-30 year olds who commonly share counter-culture values and progressive political views. Hipsters revel in witty discourse and are up on the newest creative projects and indie music. They deeply loathe anything mainstream, including media and advertisements. In some ways, they are bohemian in a refined, urban-chic way, as they are non-conformists who express a fine appreciation for art.[3]

9) Gram It–Shortened phrase meaning to use Instagram to capture a moment.

10) Hashtag–A hashtag, or what prior generations know as the "pound" sign, is used across certain social media channels to demarcate a word or short phrase in relation to a social media post. The hashtag makes that post searchable, enabling everyone to find what has been shared.

11) IRL–An acronym first used by video gamers, IRL stands for "In Real Life" and is used to distinguish the difference between an interaction happening online or in waking life; i.e. I forgot to water my plants today IRL, but my Farmville garden is thriving.

12) Give Zero Fucks–To not care or to not be bothered on any level by someone or something.

13) Bye Felicia–Originally from the 1995 comedy *Friday*, Bye Felicia is a way to dismissively say goodbye to someone that you do not care about.[4]

14) She's Basic/Basic Bitch–A pejorative phrase typically used to describe an American woman who subscribes to anything mainstream and sensationalized. Online tests will assess someone's level of "basic-ness" by asking comedic questions such as "Are your go-to desserts frozen yogurt or cupcakes?" "Do you own paraphernalia with the phrasing 'Keep Calm and ____'?" "Are you obsessed with barre-method, yoga, or Zumba?" "Have you done a juice-cleanse?" "Is Pumpkin Spice anything during the fall your favorite flavor?"

15) Ratchet–A pejorative phrase typically used to describe an American woman who is ghetto, nasty, rude, and obnoxious. This woman will more than likely always find a way to create drama.

16) Resting Bitch Face (RBF)–An unintentionally mean, snobby, or bitchy facial expression when one has a relaxed, expressionless visage.[5]

17) ICYMI–Stands for "In Case You Missed It" and is used with a hashtag (see definition) to describe past social media posts that are still relevant.

18) On Fleek–Made popular after Peaches Monroee shared a 6-second Vine video enthusiastically describing her eyebrows, the phrase means "on point," or representing a state of flawlessness or perfection (e.g. I loved Ashley's party dress and matching stilettos. Her style was on fleek!).

19) Slut-Shaming–A form of social stigma that punishes women for their real or presumed sexual activity. Mainly girls and women are called sluts for breaking traditional expectations as it relates to sexuality.

20) (Internet) Trolls–One who will deliberately post incendiary messages online via community board or through a comment, in a manner to provoke disruption, hostility, and discord.

21) Fat-Shaming–Poking fun at a person who is overweight or who does not fit the traditional standard of thinness. This may even include people who lead healthy lifestyles.

22) Thin-Shaming–Poking fun at a person who is naturally thin, as a counter-response to thin-madness and the fixation on thinness that's bred into our everyday lives.

ENDNOTES

Introduction

[1] Samantha Allen, "Millennials Are the Gayest Generation," *The Daily Beast*, March 31, 2015, http://www.thedailybeast.com/articles/2015/03/31/millennials-are-the-gayest-generation.html.

[2] Marc Prensky, "Digital Natives, Digital Immigrants," *On The Horizon* 9, no. 5 (October 2001).

1. It's Complicated

[1] Aaron Smith and Monica Anderson, "5 facts about online dating," *Pew Research Center*, April 20, 2015, http://www.pewresearch.org/fact-tank/2015/04/20/5-facts-about-online-dating/. The quoted numbers are listed under the fifth fact.

[2] Kate Santich, "Dating in the digital age-not dead, but definitely different," *Orlando Sentinel*, February 28, 2014. Sociologist Ida Cook is quoted in the fourth paragraph.

[3] "The Decline of Marriage and Rise of New Families," *Pew Research Center's Social & Demographic Trends Project,* November 18, 2010, http://www.pewsocialtrends.org/2010/11/18/v-children/.

[4] *The Paradox of Choice,* accessed January 18, 2016, http://www.ted.com/talks/barry_schwartz_on_the_paradox_of_choice?language=en.

[5] Aaron Smith and Maeve Duggan, "Online Dating & Relationships," *Pew Research Center,* October 21, 2013, http://www.pewinternet.org/2013/10/21/online-dating-relationships/.

[6] Kate Hakala, "20-Somethings Have Invented a New Relationship Status, and It's Called 'Dating Partner,'" *Connections.Mic,* February 20, 2015, http://mic.com/articles/110942/20-somethings-have-invented-a-new-relationship-status-and-it-s-called-dating-partner#.H1P2g7VH3.

2. Cat-titude of Gratitude

[1] "Pet Statistics," *ASPCA,* accessed January 25, 2016, https://www.aspca.org/animal-homelessness/shelter-intake-and-surrender/pet-statistics.

[2] Tim Kreider, "A Man and His Cat," *The New York Times,* August 1, 2014. This article was published in The Opinion Pages, or Opinionator.

[3] Other Celebricats not mentioned above include Meow, Maru, Colonel Meow, Sam, Matilda, Shironeko, Snoopy the Cat, Hamilton, Monty, Cole and Marmalade, Honey Bee, Venus, Garfi, Lazarus, Bayne, Zarathustra, Kitler, Fukumaru, Lilu, Sockington, Henri, Skifcha, Pudge, Luna the Fashion Kitty, Princess Monster Truck, and Sir Stuffington.

[4] "Caturday" refers to the practice of posting cat memes, or LOLcats, to 4chan (an imageboard forum-formatted website that has shaped much of internet culture) on Saturdays. The term is now also a tag for cat-related posts on canihas.cheezburger.com, and is also the title for the popular cat-devoted blog caturday.tumblr.com.

[5] Pusheen the Cat is a cartoon cat created by artist/blogger/author Clair Belton. The Pusheen blog can be found at pusheen.com, and Belton's other works can be found on her personal art blog clairetonic.tumblr.com

[6] Chelsea Marshall, "82 Astounding Facts About Cats," March 26, 2014,
http://www.buzzfeed.com/chelseamarshall/meows#.nyAabqxRe. Fact 73.

[7] Dovas, "My Adopted Cat Is The Best Climbing Partner Ever," *Bored Panda,* February 24, 2014,

http://www.boredpanda.com/adopted-cat-climbing-partner-craig-armstrong-millie/.

3. HOA to DOA: Getting out of Debt is the New American Dream

[1] TransUnion Newsroom, "New TransUnion Study Finds Student Loan Impact May Be Overblown," *TransUnion.* May 13, 2015, http://newsroom.transunion.com/new-transunion-study-finds-student-loan-impact-may-be-overblown. The reported figure can be found in the second paragraph of the subsection "Rapid Rise in Student Loans." The complete study can be obtained from the TransUnion website.

[2] Janet Lorin, "Borrowers Fall Further Behind on $1.3 Trillion in Student Loans," *Bloomberg Business*, August 13, 2015.

[3] Cecillia Barr, "Students & Debt." See the fourth paragraph of the subsection titled "Trends in Student Loans."

[4] Carly Stockwell, "Same as it ever was: Top 10 most popular college majors," *USA Today,* October 26, 2014.

[5] Adecco, "STEM skills drive innovation," *Adecco USA*, 2015, http://www.adeccousa.com/employers/resources/Pages/infographic-stem-skills-are-driving-innovation.aspx, (accessed November 16, 2015).

[6] Tom Dellner, *Massive Cutbacks to Public Colleges and Universities Underscore Need for Alternatives in Higher Education,* California

Southern University,
http://www.calsouthern.edu/content/articles/massive-cutbacks-to-public-colleges-and-universities-underscore-need-for-alternatives-in-higher-education/ (April 19, 2011).

[7] Kim Clark, "The Great Recession's Toll on Higher Education," *US News & Work Report,* September 10, 2010.

[8] College Board, "Trends in College Pricing 2015" (Annual Report, New York, 2015), 17.

[9] Wells Fargo Bank, "2014 Wells Fargo Millennial Study," 1.
[10] "Pros and Cons of Student Loan Consolidation for Federal Loans," *Debt.org,* accessed January 18, 2016, https://www.debt.org/students/pros-and-cons-of-student-loan-consolidation/.

[11] Federal Reserve Bank of New York, "Quarterly Report on Household Debt and Credit, February 2015" (Quarterly Report, New York, 2015), 2. See the second bullet under "Student Loans, Credit Cards, and Auto Loans."

[12] Christine DiGangi, "Does Debt Define the New American Dream?," *Credit.com,* accessed January 18, 2016, http://blog.credit.com/2013/09/debt-new-american-dream/.

[13] Robert R. Callis and Melissa Kresin, "Residential Vacancies and Homeownership in the Third Quarter 2015" (Quarterly Report, US

Department of Commerce, US Census Bureau, Washington, D.C., 2015), 4. See Table 3.

[14] Meta Brown, Sydnee Caldwell, and Sarah Sutherland, "Just Released: Young Student Loan Borrowers Remained on the Sidelines of the Housing Market in 2013," *Liberty Street Economics* (blog), *Federal Reserve Bank of New York,* May 13, 2014, http://libertystreeteconomics.newyorkfed.org/2014/05/just-released-young-student-loan-borrowers-remained-on-the-sidelines-of-the-housing-market-in-2013.html#.Vk6ib9-rT-Z. See the chart entitled "Proportion with Home-Secured Debt at Age 30.

[15] "What's Considered to Be a Good Debt-to-Income (DTI) Ratio?," *Investopedia*, accessed January 18, 2016, http://www.investopedia.com/ask/answers/081214/whats-considered-be-good-debttoincome-dti-ratio.asp.

[16] Bill McColl, "Millennials won't die broke," *Yahoo! Finance,* December 10, 2014, http://finance.yahoo.com/blogs/hot-stock-minute/millennials-won-t-die-broke-140027954.html.

[17] David Leonhardt, "What Students Don't Know About Their Loans," *The New York Times,* December 10, 2014.

[18] Heather Jarvis, "Pay as you Earn is Even Hotter Than Income Based Repayment," *Heather Jarvis: Student Loan Expert* (blog), January 7, 2013, http://askheatherjarvis.com/blog/pay-as-you-earn-hotter-than-IBR. All facts and figures listed in this section can be found in this source.

[19] Tamara Krause, "Being a Student Loan Cosigner Can Be Risky," *EStudentLoan*, April 8, 2014, http://www.estudentloan.com/blog/being-student-loan-cosigner-can-be-risky.

4. Quarter Life Crisis

[1] Oliver Robinson, Gordon Wright, and Jonathan Smith, "The holistic phase model of early adult crisis," *Journal of Adult Development* 20: (2013): 27-37.

[2] Amelia Hill, "The quarterlife crisis: young, insecure and depressed," *The Guardian,* May 5, 2011. Gumtree.com is a trading and advertising website, and any original documentation released by them concerning this survey could not be found.

[3] Bensinger, DuPont & Associates, "Depression and Work: The Impact of Depression on Different Generations of Employees" (White Paper, Chicago, 2015), 3.

[4] Brooke Bonatone, "Why are so many millennials depressed? A therapist points the finger at Mom and Dad.," *The Washington Post*, January 6, 2014.

[5] Laurence Steinberg, "The Case for Delayed Adulthood," *The New York Times*, September 19, 2014, http://www.nytimes.com/2014/09/21/opinion/sunday/the-case-for-delayed-adulthood.html.

[6] Alice Stapleton, "Under Pressure: As a Millennial experiencing the Quarter Life Crisis," *welldoing.org*, August 11, 2014, http://welldoing.org/article/pressure-life-millennial-experiencing-quarter-life-crisis. Direct quotation from the beginning of the fourth paragraph.

[7] Wells Fargo Bank, "2014 Wells Fargo Millennial Study" (Study Report, San Francisco, 2014), 1.

[8] Erin Chack, "25 Signs You're Almost 25," *buzzfeed.com*, October 20, 2014, http://www.buzzfeed.com/erinchack/25-signs-youre-almost-25#.urkWz3bva. Reason number 10.

[9] Paul Angone, "25 Signs You're Having a Quarter Life Crisis," *All Groan Up*, 2014, http://allgroanup.com/adult/25-signs-quarter-life-crisis/. The actual date of this post is unclear, so citation reflects the year listed in the copyright. This quote will likely appear in Angone's book *101 Secrets for your Twenties,* or his upcoming new book *All Groan Up: Searching for Self, Faith, and a Freaking Job!*

5. Check Your Privilege

[1] Carol M. Liebler, "Me(di)a Culpa?: The "Missing White Woman Syndrome" and Media Self-Critique" 3, no. 4 (November 17, 2010): 549–65.

[2] "Checking My Privilege: Character as the Basis of Privilege," *The Princeton Tory*, accessed January 19, 2016,

http://theprincetontory.com/main/checking-my-privilege-character-as-the-basis-of-privilege/

[3] Darnell Hunt and Ana-Christina Ramón, "2015 Hollywood Diversity Report: Flipping the Script" (Ralph J. Bunche Center for African American Studies at UCLA, February 25, 2015).

[4] Malcolm Gladwell, *Blink: The Power of Thinking without Thinking*, 1st Back Bay trade pbk. ed (New York: Back Bay Books, 2007).

[5] Michael Nam, "Unarmed Black People Twice as Likely to Be Killed by Cops As White People, Says Report," *DiversityInc*, June 8, 2015, http://www.diversityinc.com/news/unarmed-black-people-twice-as-likely-to-be-killed-by-cops-as-white-people-says-report/.

[6] *Louis CK: Chewed Up*, Directed by Shannon Hartman and Louis CK, performed by Louis CK, Berklee Performance Center, Boston, March 1, 2008. The quoted segment is called "On Being White."

[7] Dina Rickman, "The Truth behind Norway's 'First Child Wedding,'" *i100*, accessed January 19, 2016, http://i100.independent.co.uk/article/the-truth-behind-norways-first-child-wedding--lyHKZMEaBg.

[8] *Gender-Based Violence*, http://www.halftheskymovement.org/issues/gender-based-violence (accessed November 21, 2015).

[9] Kareem Abdul-Jabbar, "The Terrorist Attacks Are Not About Religion," *Time*, January 9, 2015

[10] Matthew W. Brault, "Americans With Disabilities: 2010, Household Economic Studies" (Current Population Report, US Department of Commerce, US Census Bureau, Washington, D.C., 2010), 12. See the subsection "poverty status."

[11] Liz Szabo, "Cost of Not Caring: Stigma Set in Stone," *USA TODAY*, June 25, 2014, http://www.usatoday.com/story/news/nation/2014/06/25/stigma-of-mental-illness/9875351/.

6. I Can't Stand the Rain

[1] "Serious Mental Illness (SMI) Among U.S. Adults," accessed January 25, 2016, http://www.nimh.nih.gov/health/statistics/prevalence/serious-mental-illness-smi-among-us-adults.shtml.

[2] "Depression," *Mental Health America*, accessed January 19, 2016, http://www.mentalhealthamerica.net/conditions/depression.

[3] "WHO | Background of SUPRE," *WHO*, accessed January 19, 2016, http://www.who.int/mental_health/prevention/suicide/background/en/.

4 Ashley Fants, Lindsey Knight, and Kevin Wang, *A closer look: How many Newtown-like school shootings since Sandy Hook?*, CNN, http://edition.cnn.com/2014/06/11/us/school-shootings-cnn-number/ (June 19, 2014).

5 Sharon Jayson, "Who's feeling stressed? Young adults, new survey shows," *USA Today*, February 7, 2013.

6 *Confessions of a Depressed Comic*, accessed January 19, 2016, https://www.ted.com/talks/kevin_breel_confessions_of_a_depressed_comic?language=en

7 Leeds University Union, *Mental Health: It's Time To Talk*, accessed January 19, 2016, https://www.youtube.com/watch?v=kYwyzkb67pA.

8 "Depression," *World Health Organization Media Centre*, October 2015, http://www.who.int/mediacentre/factsheets/fs369/en/.

9 "Facts & Statistics," *Anxiety and Depression Association of America*, September 2014, http://www.adaa.org/about-adaa/press-room/facts-statistics.

10 "'Myth-Conceptions,' or Common Fabrications, Fibs, and Folklore About Anxiety | Anxiety and Depression Association of America, ADAA," accessed January 28, 2016,

http://www.adaa.org/understanding-anxiety/myth-conceptions. See myth no. 8.

[11] Margarita Tartakovsky and M. S. Associate Editor ~ 3 min read, "The Biggest Myths About Girls with ADHD," *Psych Central.com*, December 23, 2012, http://psychcentral.com/blog/archives/2012/12/23/the-biggest-myths-about-girls-with-adhd/.

[12] "Facts About ASDs," *CDC - Facts about Autism Spectrum Disorders - NCBDDD*, accessed January 25, 2016, http://www.cdc.gov/ncbddd/autism/facts.html.

[13] Kathleen Doheny, "8 Myths About Bipolar Disorder," *WebMD.com*, August 1, 2008, http://www.webmd.com/bipolar-disorder/features/8-myths-about-bipolar-disorder. See page 2, under "Bipolar Myth no. 3."

[14] Robert O. Friedel, "Myths About Borderline Personality Disorder," *Borderline Personality Disorder Demystified*, 2012, (accessed November 23, 2015), http://www.bpddemystified.com/what-is-bpd/myths-about-borderline-disorder/. See no. 2.

[15] "Debunking Eating Disorder Myths - Allianceforeatingdisorders.com," accessed January 19, 2016, http://www.allianceforeatingdisorders.com/portal/debunking-eating-disorder-myths#.Vp21ShjytTI.

[16] "Five Common Myths About Depression," *Forbes*, accessed January 19, 2016, http://www.forbes.com/sites/daviddisalvo/2014/08/12/five-common-myths-about-depression/.

[17] Beth W. Orenstein, "8 Common Myths About OCD," *Everday HEALTH*, October 13, 2011, http://www.everydayhealth.com/anxiety/8-common-myths-about-ocd.aspx. See myth no. 2.

[18] "Nine Myths About Panic Disorder - Panic Disorder - Anxiety," accessed January 19, 2016, http://www.healthcentral.com/anxiety/c/1443/116411/panic-disorder/.

[19] "PTSD Myths or Myths of Posttraumatic Stress Disorder," *PTSD Alliance*, accessed January 19, 2016, http://www.ptsdalliance.org/common-myths/.

[20] "Myths and Facts About Schizophrenia — NEOMED," Landing Page One, accessed January 19, 2016, http://www.neomed.edu/academics/bestcenter/helpendstigma/myths-and-facts-about-schizophrenia.

7. All in a Day's Work

[1] Dan Schawbel, "3rd Annual Study on the State of Gen Y Gen X and Baby Boomer Workers," *Millennial Branding*, November 19,

2014, http://millennialbranding.com/2014/3rd-annual-study-state-gen-gen-baby-boomer-workers/. Direct quotation is in the sixth and seventh paragraph under the subsection "Highlights from the report include:".

[2] Upwork, "The 2015 Millennials Workforce Majority Report," *Elance-oDesk and Millennial Branding.* October 2014, http://www.slideshare.net/oDesk/2015-millennial-majority-workforce (accessed December 5, 2015). See slide 25.

[3] Todd Sorensen, "Data on Millennials & How Much Time They Spend Working," October 6, 2015.

[4] "Millennials Surpass Gen Xers as the Largest Generation in U.S. Labor Force | Pew Research Center," accessed January 19, 2016, http://www.pewresearch.org/fact-tank/2015/05/11/millennials-surpass-gen-xers-as-the-largest-generation-in-u-s-labor-force/.

[5] Upwork, "The 2015 Millennials Workforce Majority Report." See footnote 18.

[6] Glassdoor, "Top HR Statistics: the latest stats for HR & Recruiting Pros," *Glassdoor,* https://www.glassdoor.com/employers/popular-topics/hr-stats.htm, (accessed December 6, 2015). See the eighth item under subsection "Recruiting."

[7] "Banner - Australian Boot Trade Employees⊠: Museum Victoria," accessed January 25, 2016, http://museumvictoria.com.au/learning-federation/trade-union-banners/banner---australian-boot-trade-employees-federation-ballarat-branch-circa-1905/.

[8] Louis Jacobson, "Does the 8-Hour Day and the 40-Hour Week Come from Henry Ford, or Labor Unions?," *Politifact*, September 9, 2015, http://www.politifact.com/truth-o-meter/statements/2015/sep/09/viral-image/does-8-hour-day-and-40-hour-come-henry-ford-or-lab/.

[9] Seth Stevenson, "Don't Go to Work: The Management that lets workers do whatever they want, as long as they get things done," *Slate*, May 11, 2014, http://www.slate.com/articles/business/psychology_of_management/2014/05/best_buy_s_rowe_experiment_can_results_only_work_environments_actually_be.single.html.

[10] University of Minnesota, "Flexible schedules and results-oriented work environments reduce work-family conflict and turnover, U of M researchers find," April 6, 2011, http://discover.umn.edu/news/arts-humanities/flexible-schedules-and-results-oriented-work-environments-reduce-work-family.

[11] Nicholas Bloom, "To Raise Productivity, Let More Employees Work From Home," *Harvard Business Review*, January-February 2014. Page numbers not provided as this article can be accessed online at https://hbr.org/2014/01/to-raise-productivity-let-more-employees-work-from-home.

[12] Richard Feloni, "Inside Zappos CEO Tony Hsieh's Radical Management Experiment That Prompted 14% of Employees to Quit," May 16, 2015, http://www.businessinsider.com/tony-hsieh-zappos-holacracy-management-experiment-2015-5

[13] Jeanne C. Meister and Karie Willyerd, "Mentoring Millennials," *Harvard Business Review*, accessed January 19, 2016, https://hbr.org/2010/05/mentoring-millennials.

[14] Tommy Caldwell, "GMOs Aren't That Bad, But Monsanto Is the Worst | VICE | Canada," *VICE*, June 6, 2013, http://www.vice.com/en_ca/read/mutant-food-and-the-march-against-monsanto.

[15] James Covert, "'Sex Slave' Led to Ouster of American Apparel CEO | New York Post," January 20, 2014, http://nypost.com/2014/06/20/american-apparel-ceo-ouster-linked-to-sex-slave-case/.

[16] Jeff DeGraff, "Digital Natives vs. Digital Immigrants | Jeff DeGraff," *Huffington Post*, September 7, 2014, http://www.huffingtonpost.com/jeff-degraff/digital-natives-vs-digita_b_5499606.html

[17] Anonymous, Gen-X vs Gen-Y: Cultural Differences in the Workplace, 2015.

[18] Margaret Rouse, "What Is SMAC (social, Mobile, Analytics and Cloud)? - Definition from WhatIs.com," *SearchCIO*, July 2014, http://searchcio.techtarget.com/definition/SMAC-social-mobile-analytics-and-cloud.

[19] Jeanne C. Meister and Karie Willyerd, "Mentoring Millennials," *Harvard Business Review*, May 2010, https://hbr.org/2010/05/mentoring-millennials.

"HR Statistics and Best Practices," *Glassdoor*, accessed January 19, 2016, https://www.glassdoor.com/employers/popular-topics/hr-stats.htm.

[20] "Glassdoor.com Traffic and Demographic Statistics by Quantcast," accessed January 19, 2016, https://www.quantcast.com/glassdoor.com#trafficCard

[21] Laura Vanderkam, "Here's Why an Unlimited Vacation Policy May Be Too Good to Be True," *Fortune*, October 3, 2015, http://fortune.com/2015/10/03/unlimited-vacation-policy/.

[22] Marketwatch, "Millennial Parents Are Poorest Generation in 25 Years," *New York Post*, April 29, 2015, http://nypost.com/2015/04/29/millennial-parents-are-poorest-generation-in-25-years/.

[23] Jacquelyn Smith, "The 3 Questions One CEO Hopes to Hear from Everyone He Interviews — but Hardly Ever Does," *Business Insider*,

June 15, 2015, http://www.businessinsider.com/important-interview-questions-job-candidates-forget-to-ask-2015-6.

8. The F-Word

[1] Judith Warner | Friday, March 7, and 2014, "Fact Sheet: The Women's Leadership Gap," *Name*, March 7, 2014, https://www.americanprogress.org/issues/women/report/2014/03/07/85457/fact-sheet-the-womens-leadership-gap/

[2] Ravi Somaiya, "Rolling Stone Article on Rape at University of Virginia Failed All Basics, Report Says," *The New York Times*, April 5, 2015, http://www.nytimes.com/2015/04/06/business/media/rolling-stone-retracts-article-on-rape-at-university-of-virginia.html.

[3] Emily Bazelon, "Have We Learned Anything From the Columbia Rape Case?," *The New York Times*, May 29, 2015, http://www.nytimes.com/2015/05/29/magazine/have-we-learned-anything-from-the-columbia-rape-case.html.

[4] Sofi Sinozich and Lynn Langton, "Rape and Sexual Assault Victimization among College-Age Females, 1995-2013," *US Department of Justice, Office of Justice Programs, The Bureau of Justice Statistcs. Full Text Available at Http://www. Bjs. gov/content/pub/pdf/rsavcaf9513. Pdf*, 2014, https://assets.documentcloud.org/documents/1378364/rsavcaf9513.pdf.

[5] Richard A. Oppel Jr, "2 Teenagers Found Guilty in Steubenville, Ohio, Rape," *The New York Times*, March 17, 2013, http://www.nytimes.com/2013/03/18/us/teenagers-found-guilty-in-rape-in-steubenville-ohio.html.

[6] Jake New, "Colleges across Country Adopting Affirmative Consent Sexual Assault Policies," *Inside Higher Ed*, October 17, 2014, https://www.insidehighered.com/news/2014/10/17/colleges-across-country-adopting-affirmative-consent-sexual-assault-policies.

[7] "How Millennials Use and Control Social Media," *American Press Institute*, March 15, 2015, https://www.americanpressinstitute.org/publications/reports/survey-research/millennials-social-media/.

[8] Rob Bliss Creative, *10 Hours of Walking in NYC as a Woman*, accessed January 24, 2016, https://www.youtube.com/watch?v=b1XGPvbWn0A.

[9] Rachel Zarrell BuzzFeed News Reporter, "#DudesGreetingDudes Is One Guy's Flawless Takedown Of Catcalling," *BuzzFeed*, November 5, 2014, http://www.buzzfeed.com/rachelzarrell/dudes-greeting-dudes.

[10] "Case Study: Always #LikeAGirl," *D&AD*, accessed January 24, 2016, http://www.dandad.org/en/case-study-always-likeagirl/.

[11] Beth Elderkin, "These Are the 'Women Against Feminism,'" *The Daily Dot*, August 3, 2014, http://www.dailydot.com/lifestyle/women-against-feminism-tumblr/.

[15] Malala Yousafzai and Christina Lamb, *I Am Malala: The Girl Who Stood up for Education and Was Shot by the Taliban*, First edition (New York, NY: Little, Brown, & Company, 2013).

[16] "Girls' Education" (The World Bank, December 3, 2014), www.wordlbank.org.

[17] "Emma Watson Gender Equality Is Your Issue Too | UN Women – Headquarters," *UN Women*, September 20, 2014, http://www.unwomen.org/en/news/stories/2014/9/emma-watson-gender-equality-is-your-issue-too.

[18] Eleanor Smeal, "The Feminist Factor," *Ms. Magazine*, Winter 2013, http://www.msmagazine.com/winter2013/feministfactor.asp.

[19] "Parliament Passes Anti-Pornography Law," accessed January 24, 2016, http://www.parliament.go.ug/new/index.php/about-parliament/parliamentary-news/325-parliament-passes-anti-pornography-law.

[20] Lizzie Dearden, "'Women Should Not Laugh in Public,' Says

Turkey's Deputy PM," *The Independent*, July 29, 2014, http://www.independent.co.uk/news/world/europe/women-should-not-laugh-in-public-says-turkeys-deputy-prime-minister-in-morality-speech-9635526.html.

[21] Leanne Smith, "Should School Dress Codes Permit Yoga Pants, Leggings and Stretch Pants? Take Our Poll," *MLive.com*, August 18, 2015, http://www.mlive.com/news/jackson/index.ssf/2015/08/should_school_dress_codes_perm.html.

[22] "Iranian Women Still Banned from Stadiums - Al-Monitor: The Pulse of the Middle East," *Al-Monitor*, accessed January 24, 2016, http://www.al-monitor.com/pulse/originals/2014/06/iran-womens-volleyball-barred-entry.html.

[23] Erika Eichelberger and Molly Redden, "In Hobby Lobby Case, the Supreme Court Chooses Religion over Science," *Mother Jones*, June 30, 2014, http://www.motherjones.com/politics/2014/06/supreme-court-hobby-lobby-decision.

[24] Gabriele Steinhauser and Inti Landauro, "European Human Rights Court Upholds France's Burqa Ban," *Wall Street Journal*, July 1, 2014, sec. World, http://www.wsj.com/articles/european-human-rights-court-upholds-frances-burqa-ban-1404210496.

[25] "IS RED LIPSTICK 'TOO SEXY' FOR KIDS' TV?," *BIRDEE*, January 30, 2014, http://birdeemag.com/red-lipstick-sexy-kids-tv/.

[26] Ladane Nasseri, "Iranian Café Work Ban to Leave Women Jobless, Official Says - Bloomberg Business," September 3, 2014, http://www.bloomberg.com/news/articles/2014-09-03/iran-vp-says-banning-women-from-caf-work-will-boost-joblessness.

[27] Staff and agencies, "Microsoft CEO Satya Nadella: Women, Don't Ask for a Raise," *The Guardian*, October 9, 2014, sec. Technology, http://www.theguardian.com/technology/2014/oct/10/microsoft-ceo-satya-nadella-women-dont-ask-for-a-raise.

[28] *Jessica's Feminized Atmosphere*, 2014, http://www.cc.com/video-clips/5ndnit/the-daily-show-with-jon-stewart-jessica-s-feminized-atmosphere.

[29] SYED RASHID HUSAIN, "Saudis Told Not to Marry Women from Pakistan, 3 Other States," August 6, 2014, http://www.dawn.com/news/1123519.

[30] Brooke, "Why I Refused to Put a Shirt on For Shape," *Brooke: Not On a Diet*, May 2, 2014, http://brookenotonadiet.com/2014/05/02/refuse-put-shirt/.

[31] Phil Savage, "Hearthstone Tournament Explains Why Women Aren't Allowed to Play [updated]," *PC Gamer*, July 1, 2014, http://www.pcgamer.com//hearthstone-tournament/.

[32] "Christian School Complains 8-Year-Old Girl Isn't Girly Enough," March 25, 2014, http://www.cbsnews.com/news/christian-school-complains-8-year-old-girl-isnt-girly-enough/.

[33] Meghann Myers, "Navy Boots Sailor over Her Natural Hairstyle," *USA TODAY*, August 22, 2014, http://www.usatoday.com/story/news/nation/2014/08/22/navy-sailor-discharge-disobeying-hair-rules/14430013/.

[34] Meghan Holohan, "Victoria's Secret Store Bans Mom from Breastfeeding," *TODAY.com*, January 21, 2014, http://www.today.com/parents/victorias-secret-store-bans-mom-breastfeeding-2D11968546.

9. Give it to Me Straight

[1] "Growing Support for Gay Marriage: Changed Minds and Changing Demographics," *Pew Research Center for the People and the Press*, March 20, 2013, http://www.people-press.org/2013/03/20/growing-support-for-gay-marriage-changed-minds-and-changing-demographics/.

[2] Maureen McCarty, "President Obama Reiterates Support for Marriage Equality During State of the Union," *Human Rights Campaign*, January 20, 2015, http://www.hrc.org/blog/president-obama-reiterates-support-for-marriage-equality-during-state-of-th/.

3 Eliana Dockterman, "White House Supports Efforts to Ban 'Conversion Therapy' for Youth," *Time*, April 8, 2015, http://time.com/3814732/white-house-conversion-therapy-youth/.

4 Laura E. Durso and Gary J. Gates, "Serving Our Youth: Findings from a National Survey of Services Providers Working with Lesbian, Gay, Bisexual and Transgender Youth Who Are Homeless or at Risk of Becoming Homeless," 2012, http://escholarship.org/uc/item/80x75033.pdf.

5 "Gay and Transgender Youth Homelessness by the Numbers," *Center for American Progress*, June 21, 2010, https://www.americanprogress.org/issues/lgbt/news/2010/06/21/798 0/gay-and-transgender-youth-homelessness-by-the-numbers/.

6 Samantha Allen, "Millennials Are the Gayest Generation," *The Daily Beast*, March 31, 2015, http://www.thedailybeast.com/articles/2015/03/31/millennials-are-the-gayest-generation.html.

7 "Changing Attitudes on Gay Marriage," *Pew Research Center's Religion & Public Life Project*, July 29, 2015, http://www.pewforum.org/2015/07/29/graphics-slideshow-changing-attitudes-on-gay-marriage/.

8 Michael Dimock, Carroll Doherty, and Jocelyn Kiley, "Growing

Support for Gay Marriage: Changed Minds and Changing Demographics," *Gen* 10 (2013): 1965–80.

[9] Bianca Slota, "Transgender Vt. Teen Wants Genderless Bathrooms in School - USATODAY.com," *WCAX*, August 28, 2009, http://usatoday30.usatoday.com/news/education/2009-08-31-gender-bathrooms_N.htm.

[10] Sarah Wheaton, "Latest White House Feature: Gender-Neutral Restroom," *POLITICO*, April 8, 2015, http://social.politico.com/story/2015/04/white-house-gender-neutral-bathroom-116779.html.

[11] Eytan Bakshy, "Showing Support for Marriage Equality on Facebook," *Facebook*, March 29, 2013, https://www.facebook.com/notes/facebook-data-science/showing-support-for-marriage-equality-on-facebook/10151430548593859/.

[12] Melanie Tannenbaum, "Will Changing Your Facebook Profile Picture Do Anything for Marriage Equality? - Scientific American Blog Network," *Scientific American*, March 28, 2013, http://blogs.scientificamerican.com/psysociety/marriage-equality-and-social-proof/.

[13] *See The Real Me – Jazz Jennings: Being Your True Self | Clean & Clear*, 2015, https://www.youtube.com/watch?v=vyNZXQ136oI.

[14] Obergefell v. Hodges (Supreme Court of the United States 2015).

10. Myth of the Post-Racial Society

[1] LAWRENCE OTIS GRAHAM, "Lawrence Otis Graham: I Thought Privilege Would Protect My Kids from Racism. I Was Wrong.," November 12, 2014, http://www.dallasnews.com/opinion/sunday-commentary/20141112-lawrence-otis-graham-i-thought-privilege-would-protect-my-kids-from-racism.-i-was-wrong..ece.

[2] Michael I. Norton and Samuel R. Sommers, "Whites See Racism as a Zero-Sum Game That They Are Now Losing," *Perspectives on Psychological Science* 6, no. 3 (May 1, 2011): 215–18, doi:10.1177/1745691611406922.

[3] Melanie E. L. Bush, *Everyday Forms of Whiteness: Understanding Race in a "Post-Racial" World* (Rowman & Littlefield Publishers, 2011).

[4] Kerry Burke, "Barneys Accused Me of Stealing Because I'm Black: Teen," *NY Daily News*, October 24, 2013, http://www.nydailynews.com/new-york/barneys-accused-stealing-black-teen-article-1.1493101.

[5] Jake New, "The Ugly, Racist, Deadly History of Sigma Alpha

Epsilon," *Slate*, March 13, 2015,
http://www.slate.com/articles/life/inside_higher_ed/2015/03/behind_the_chant_discrimination_at_oklahoma_s_sae_chapter_goes_deeper_than.html.

[6] Emily Badger, "12 Years of Data from New York City Suggest Stop-and-Frisk Wasn't That Effective," *The Washington Post*, August 21, 2014,
https://www.washingtonpost.com/news/wonk/wp/2014/08/21/12-years-of-data-from-new-york-city-suggest-stop-and-frisk-wasnt-that-effective/.

[7] Matt Bruenig, "The Racial Wealth Gap," *Demos*, November 5, 2013, http://www.demos.org/blog/11/5/13/racial-wealth-gap.

[8] Ary Spatig-Amerikaner, "Unequal Education," *Name*, August 22, 2012,
https://www.americanprogress.org/issues/education/report/2012/08/22/29002/unequal-education/.

[9] "Freedmen's Savings and Trust Company (1865-1874) | The Black Past: Remembered and Reclaimed," accessed January 9, 2016,
http://www.blackpast.org/aah/freedmen-s-savings-and-trust-company-1865-1874.

[10] "Future of Fair Housing: How We Got Here," *The Leadership Conference on Civil and Human Rights*, accessed January 9, 2016,
http://www.civilrights.org/publications/reports/fairhousing/historic

al.html.

[11] Debbie Gruenstein Bocian, Keith S. Ernst, and Wei Li, "Unfair Lending: The Effect of Race and Ethnicity on the Price of Subprime Mortgages," May 31, 2006, www.responsiblelending.org.

[12] Brave New Films, *Racism Is Real • BRAVE NEW FILMS*, accessed January 9, 2016, https://www.youtube.com/watch?v=fTcSVQJ2h8g.

[13] David Goldman, "Total 2008 Job Loss: 2.6 Million - Jan. 9, 2009," *CNN*, January 9, 2009, http://money.cnn.com/2009/01/09/news/economy/jobs_december/.

[14] Yesha Callahan, "What's in a Name? Man Changes Name From 'José' to 'Joe,' Gains Job Interviews - The Root," *The Root*, September 4, 2014, http://www.theroot.com/blogs/the_grapevine/2014/09/what_s_in_a_name_man_changes_name_from_jos_to_joe_gains_job_interviews.html.

[15] Michael Luo, "'Whitening' the Résumé," *The New York Times*, December 5, 2009, http://www.nytimes.com/2009/12/06/weekinreview/06Luo.html.

[16] Eve Tahmincioglu, "Like It or Not, Name Can Impact Your Career," *Msnbc.com*, November 23, 2009, http://www.nbcnews.com/id/34063244/ns/business-careers/t/it-or-

not-name-can-impact-your-career/.

[17] Lilly Workneh, "16-Year-Old Amandla Stenberg Schools Everyone On Cultural Appropriation," *The Huffington Post*, April 14, 2015, http://www.huffingtonpost.com/2015/04/14/amandla-stenberg-cultural_n_7064420.html.

[18] Marcus Gilmer, "Bree Newsome, Who Scaled a Pole to Take down Confederate Flag, Speaks out," *Mashable*, June 29, 2015, http://mashable.com/2015/06/29/bree-newsome-confederate-flag-comments/.

[19] Abagond, "Unarmed Black Americans Killed by Police in 2015," *Abagond*, August 2015, https://abagond.wordpress.com/2015/08/11/unarmed-black-americans-killed-by-police-in-2015/.

[20] Rich Juzwiak and Aleksander Chan, "Unarmed People of Color Killed by Police, 1999-2014," *Gawker*, December 8, 2014, http://gawker.com/unarmed-people-of-color-killed-by-police-1999-2014-1666672349.

11. All About That Bass *and* Treble

[1] Tess Koman, "If Enough Women Use #PlusSizePlease, Will Fashion Brands Listen?," *Cosmopolitan*, July 4, 2015,

http://www.cosmopolitan.com/lifestyle/news/a41473/plussizeplease-hashtag/.

[2] Stanten, Michele, "Fast Track to Sexy," *Shape*, January 2014.

[3] Isabelle Chapman, "Victoria's Secret Renames 'The Perfect Body' Campaign Slogan," *AOL.com*, November 6, 2014, http://www.aol.com/article/2014/11/06/victorias-secret-renames-the-perfect-body-campaign-slogan/20989838/.

[4] The Dear Kate Team, "The Perfect Body," *Dear Kate*, October 31, 2014, http://www.dearkates.com/blogs/diary/15637197-the-perfect-body.

[6] Dan Schawbel, "10 New Findings About The Millennial Consumer," *Forbes*, January 20, 2015, http://www.forbes.com/sites/danschawbel/2015/01/20/10-new-findings-about-the-millennial-consumer/.

[7] Sarah Wasilak, "Lane Bryant's #ImNoAngel Campaign Is Trying to Redefine Sexy — but Does It Work?," *POPSUGAR Fashion*, April 6, 2015, http://www.popsugar.com/fashion/Lane-Bryant-Im-Angel-Campaign-37224250.

[8] Jean Kilbourne, "Killing Us Softly: Advertising's Image of

Women," accessed January 9, 2016,
http://www.jeankilbourne.com/videos/.

[9] Wade, T.D., Keski-Rahkonen A., and Hudson J., *Textbook of Psychiatric Epidemiology*, ed. Ming T. Tsuang and Mauricio Tohen, Mauricio, 3rd ed (Chichester, West Sussex ; Hoboken, NJ: Wiley-Blackwell, 2011).

[10] Heather Chen, "Waist Wars: China Belly Button Challenge Gets Trending," *BBC News*, June 11, 2015,
http://www.bbc.com/news/world-asia-china-33091349.

[11] Rebecca Macatee, "Kylie Jenner Lip Challenge Produces Terrifying Results," *E! Online*, April 21, 2015,
http://www.eonline.com/news/648544/kylie-jenner-lip-challenge-produces-terrifying-results-teens-this-is-not-the-way-to-plump-your-pout.

[12] Ron Underwood, "Ugly Betty," *Zero Worship*, January 10, 2008.

[13] Lesley McKenzie, "What Mindy Kaling Wishes She'd Known as a Teenager," *Teen Vogue*, February 10, 2014,
http://www.teenvogue.com/story/mindy-kaling-advice-for-teen-girls.

[14] *Looks Aren't Everything. Believe Me, I'm a Model.*, accessed

January 9, 2016,
https://www.ted.com/talks/cameron_russell_looks_aren_t_everythi
ng_believe_me_i_m_a_model.

[15] "The Dove® Campaign for Real Beauty," accessed January 9, 2016,
http://www.dove.us/Social-Mission/campaign-for-real-beauty.aspx.

[16] SpecialKUS, *Special K ® More Than a Number*, accessed January 9,
2016, https://www.youtube.com/watch?v=TQOpjnEG4GY.

[17] BuzzFeedVideo, *What Do Strangers Think Of You?*, accessed
January 9, 2016, https://www.youtube.com/watch?v=jg-O7f_1Ngc.

[18] Mario, "BYOB - Be Your Own Beautiful - Amplify," *Amplify - A
Project of Advocates for Youth*, May 21, 2013,
http://amplifyyourvoice.org/u/marioapalmer/2013/05/21/byob-be-
your-own-beautiful/.

[19] Scott Stump, "Size-10 Model Defends Calvin Klein in 'plus Size'
Controversy," *TODAY.com*, November 11, 2014,
http://www.today.com/style/model-myla-dalbesio-calvin-klein-
using-me-groundbreaking-1D80280707.

[20] Nina Bahadur, "#EffYourBeautyStandards, This Model Has No
Use For Them," *The Huffington Post*, February 10, 2015,
http://www.huffingtonpost.com/2015/01/27/eff-your-beauty-
standards-tess-holliday_n_6554448.html.

[21] Corbin Chamberlin, "Wheelchair-Bound Blogger Warms Fashion Week Hearts," *The Daily Beast*, February 7, 2013, http://www.thedailybeast.com/articles/2013/02/07/wheelchair-bound-blogger-warms-fashion-week-hearts.html.

[22] Maggie Freleng, "Designer Puts Wheelchair in the N.Y. Fashion Mix | Womens eNews," February 12, 2014, http://womensenews.org/story/cultural-trendspopular-culture/140211/designer-puts-wheelchair-in-the-ny-fashion-mix.

[23] "'I Am a Vain Fool' Says TV Personality Who Wants No Makeup to Be the Norm," *CBC News*, November 18, 2014, http://www.cbc.ca/news/arts/tracey-spicer-australian-tv-personality-reveals-makeup-free-face-1.2839165.

12. Self(ie)-Obsessed

[1] Erica Sheftman, "What Google I/O Means for Marketers in 2014 and Beyond," *The Percolate Blog*, July 1, 2014, https://blog.percolate.com/2014/07/google-io-means-marketers-2014-beyond/.

[2] "Selfie," *Wikipedia, the Free Encyclopedia*, December 31, 2015, https://en.wikipedia.org/w/index.php?title=Selfie&oldid=697637742

[3] "Robert Cornelius' Self-Portrait: The First Ever 'Selfie' (1839)," *The Public Domain Review*, accessed January 3, 2016, http://publicdomainreview.org/collections/robert-cornelius-self-portrait-the-first-ever-selfie-1839/.

[4] Ruth Styles, "Is This the World's First Amateur Selfie? Woman Captured Her Own Image in 1900 with Kodak Box Brownie Camera," *Dailymail.co.uk*, November 19, 2013, http://www.dailymail.co.uk/femail/article-2509952/Black-white-selfies-dating-1800s-shed-light-history-self-portrait.html.

[5] Ira Kalb, "Selfies And Smartphone Video Are Changing Marketing," *Business Insider*, August 18, 2014, http://www.businessinsider.com/how-selfies-are-changing-marketing-2014-8.

[6] Kara Burney, "Why You Should Envy GoPro's Instagram Strategy (And How You Can Emulate It)," *TrackMaven*, January 14, 2015, http://trackmaven.com/blog/2015/01/why-you-should-envy-and-emulate-gopros-instagram-strategy/.

[7] Marnie Kunz, "Axe 'Kiss for Peace' Campaign Promotes International Goodwill, Social Media Style," *PSFK*, August 21, 2014, http://www.psfk.com/2014/08/axe-fragrance-social-beauty-goodwill-campaign.html.

[8] Jennifer Beese, "5 Insightful Instagram Stats You Need To Know," *Sprout Social*, January 22, 2015, http://sproutsocial.com/insights/5-

instagram-stats/.

[9] Kate Talbot, "5 Ways to Use Snapchat for Business⊠: Social Media Examiner," *Social Media Examiner*, July 28, 2015, http://www.socialmediaexaminer.com/5-ways-to-use-snapchat-for-business/.

[10] Heather Kelly, "Young Drivers Snapping 'Selfies' at the Wheel - CNN.com," *CNN*, November 6, 2013, http://www.cnn.com/2013/11/06/tech/mobile/selfies-while-driving/index.html.

[11] Max Knoblauch, "Visitors in Lake Tahoe Are Taking Too Many Bear Selfies," *Mashable*, October 27, 2014, http://mashable.com/2014/10/27/bear-selfies/.

[12] Andrea Romano, "Faux Surprise Face Is the New Duckface," *Mashable*, January 22, 2015, http://mashable.com/2015/01/22/faux-surprise-face/.

13. Waiting for My Owl

[1] Sara Bibel, "Poof! 5 Little-Known Facts About How J.K. Rowling Brought Harry Potter to Life," *Biography*, July 30, 2014, http://www.biography.com/news/jk-rowling-harry-potter-facts.

[2] Jennifer Schaffer, "18 Magical Ways 'Harry Potter' Changed Your

Life," *BuzzFeed*, December 4, 2014,
http://www.buzzfeed.com/jenniferschaffer/lumos-solem.

[3] "JK Rowling Outs Dumbledore as Gay," *BBC*, October 20, 2007,
sec. Entertainment, http://news.bbc.co.uk/2/hi/7053982.stm.

[4] "Pottermore: JK Rowling Facts and Figures," June 23, 2011, sec.
Culture, http://www.telegraph.co.uk/culture/harry-
potter/8592280/Pottermore-JK-Rowling-facts-and-figures.html.

[5] The Brilliant Mind Behind Harry Potter," *Oprah.com*, accessed
January 3, 2016,

http://www.oprah.com/oprahshow/The-Brilliant-Mind-Behind-
Harry-Potter. See page 9, paragraph 2.

[6] Ray Duggan, "JK Rowling's Depression Inspired Some of Her Most
Iconic Villains.," *Mamamia*, December 25, 2013,
http://www.mamamia.com.au/jk-rowling-depression-dementors/.

[7] Jessica Goodman, "J.K. Rowling Says We've All Been Pronouncing
Voldemort Wrong | EW.com," *Entertainment Weekly*, September
10, 2015, http://www.ew.com/article/2015/09/10/jk-rowling-
voldemort-pronunciation-wrong.

[8] David Colbert, *The Magical Worlds of Harry Potter: A Treasury of
Myths, Legends, and Fascinating Facts.* (Lumina Press, 2011).

[9] "Natalie McDonald," *Harry Potter Wiki*, accessed January 3, 2016, http://harrypotter.wikia.com/wiki/Natalie_McDonald.

[10] "Amortentia," *Harry Potter Wiki*, accessed January 3, 2016, http://harrypotter.wikia.com/wiki/Amortentia.

14. Can You Repeat That? (Millennial Slang)

[1] Henry Joost and Ariel Schulman, *Catfish*, Documentary, (2010).

[2] "Bro," *Urban Dictionary*, May 8, 2005, http://www.urbandictionary.com/define.php?term=bro.

[3] "Hipster," *Urban Dictionary*, November 22, 2007, http://www.urbandictionary.com/define.php?term=hipster.

[4] Kaitlin Reilly, "What Does 'Bye, Felicia' Mean & Why Are People Saying It All of a Sudden?," *Bustle*, December 9, 2014, http://www.bustle.com/articles/52505-what-does-bye-felicia-mean-why-are-people-saying-it-all-of-a-sudden.

[5] Miisty, "Resting Bitch Face," *Urban Dictionary*, April 1, 2011, http://www.urbandictionary.com/define.php?term=resting+bitch+face

Acknowledgements

Several people–and one very dashing cat–have inspired the creation and evolution of this book. Here we go in no particular order…

I'm eternally grateful for the love, support, and late night 2-, 3-, and 4- hour conversations I had with my mom throughout writing this book. Mom, you're a great listener, idealist, creative thinker, and the perfect shoulder to lean on. You've inspired so many of the chapters and accompanying content in this book. I'm truly lucky to know a woman who is as brilliant and adaptable to change as you are. Pat Geary, you are also on my list of inspirational women who pushed me to keep going. If it weren't for you, there would be no book number two. You challenged me when we met in that coffee shop back in 2014 to start another writing project, despite my fears.

Without your encouraging words, I never would have tried to go beyond what I was comfortable achieving. Thank you for that extra push.

To Grandma Jones, may your soul rest peacefully. You are the reason I am a writer. If it weren't for you teaching me how to read and write from day one, using your skills as an English teacher, who knows where I would have ended up. I've always admired your perseverance to keep going even when times get tough.

Mom would tell me stories of you sneaking out at night to study in a car under a street lamp because you were scared of your husband waking up and finding you. That alone has taught me to never take advantage of the opportunities we are given and to keep fighting for women's equality, especially for girls in other countries who don't have access to an education or who are scared to study just like you were, but who do it regardless. I'm so honored to have had a fighter as a role model and grandmother.

To Jehovah, my creator and best friend, I serve you in all of your glory. Through you, I have written something extraordinary and my fingers could not have been better guided. Thank you to you and your son, Jesus, for being my support, my rock, and my shepherd.

Finally, to the very dashing tuxedo cat, Mr. Kitty, who sat by my side during nights of stress (and trust me, there were many!), you are my favorite cuddle buddy and emotional support cat even if you don't help out with chores and party with Beyoncé every night…inside joke.

Next up, I want to thank the people who have helped me with some of the formatting odds and ends of this book, as well as research, to make this as awesome and unique as it is. Erin Garey you are a saint. I had a book cover design that needed formatting and you worked your PhotoShop magic–not once but twice– to make sure it was ready for print. You only requested a drink in return, but I owe you so much more for being an incredible friend. Thank you for being the kickass artist and overall cool person that you are.

A huge thanks to Healthy is the New Skinny for the awesome T-shirt you gave me so that I could sport it in my back cover photo. You have no idea how many lives you have changed and are continuing to change by teaching women to love their bodies again, and all thanks to the vision of Katie Wilcox.

Clarke, my handsome college friend who always intimidated me with your natural ability to play it cool, you're an incredibly gifted photographer and I know you will succeed beyond your wildest dreams. You nailed the photo of me on the back cover. I've never looked more amazing and it is all thanks to your awesome skills behind the lens.

Phillip, you are incredibly talented when it comes to navigating Word documents. You spent all evening letting me use your computer when mine crashed helping me format the last bit of my manuscript. You had homework to do of your own, but nonetheless worked with me until 11:00 p.m. I'm incredibly thankful and owe you a fancy twenty dollar cocktail of some sort.

Lastly, a HUGE thank you to labor economist Todd Sorensen for volunteering to pull data and research for me. As always, I'm impressed with how much of a whiz you are with stats and numbers. Plus, you're a pretty cool guy to shoot the shit with.

For my last round of thank you's, these two women will never know how much they have positively impacted my life. Mindy Kaling, you are my superhero, my ideal shopping buddy, and probably one of the fiercest comedians out there. I admire your hard work and drive. Whenever I felt as though I couldn't keep going, I thought of you and how hard you worked to make your dreams a reality. Good things don't always come easily, but if you persevere you shine. You're the perfect embodiment of that. And to the incredible Tig Notaro, I can't tell you how many times I've turned to watch you on Netflix to get me through a bad spot. I am so inspired by your tenacity and fearlessness, and can only hope to reach that level of cool by the time I die (#NoChill).

Cheers to everyone and let's keep inspiring other women around us so the next generation can be even better, stronger, and greater!